M000307718

the new evangelisation

Issues & Challenges for Catholic Schools

RICHARD M.RYMARZ

Modotti Press

AN IMPRINT OF CONNOR COURT PUBLISHING

*I dedicate this book to
my longstanding friend
and questioner,
Dr. Brian Conway*

Published in 2012 by Connor Court Publishing Pty Ltd.

Copyright © Richard Rymarz 2012

ALL RIGHTS RESERVED. This book contains material protected under International and Federal Copyright Laws and Treaties. Any unauthorized reprint or use of this material is prohibited. No part of this book may be reproduced or transmitted in any form or by any means, electronic or mechanical, including photocopying, recording, or by any information storage and retrieval system without express written permission from the publisher.

Connor Court Publishing Pty Ltd.
PO Box 1
Ballan VIC 3342
sales@connorcourt.com
www.connorcourt.com

ISBN: 9781921421617 (pbk.)

Cover design by Ian James

Printed in Australia

TABLE OF CONTENTS

Preface

The genesis of much of the thinking in this book can be traced back to an exchange between a close friend and myself nearly thirty years ago. At the time, we were university students heavily involved with the Catholic student group, the Newman Society, at both local and national levels. We had both graduated from Catholic schools. In conversation, my friend unexpectedly asked: "What would we do if a person came to us interested in Catholicism, wanting to find out how he could learn more, with a view to becoming a Catholic?" It was, and still is, a good question. The Catholicism that we lived in the early 1980s was not oriented towards evangelisation. We lived with a hard-to-articulate sense that evangelisation was not something modern Catholics engaged in; rather, evangelisation was a manifestation of a bygone and superseded era. This was, after all, a time where the Church was still in the turmoil of the post-conciliar era and was, in many ways, re-orientating itself. In this atmosphere, evangelisation was not something that was at the forefront of Catholic consciousness. In the terms of Avery Dulles, it was an era where "religious dialogue replace[d] missionary proclamation."[1]

As we tussled with the question, we soon became aware that what our hypothetical enquirer wanted was not a lecture, or a book, or readings. More important was personal witness, and an encounter with a vibrant community of faith – a place to see the Holy Spirit alive and at work. I reflected that we needed something like the fellowship evident in the university Evangelical Union. Here were people who seemed to be alive with the love of Christ; a little effusive perhaps,

---

1 Avery Dulles, *The New World of Faith.* (Huntington, IN: Our Sunday Visitor, 2000), 107.

but nonetheless sincere. The Evangelicals were also very keen to bring others into a deeper relationship with Christ or, as we termed it then, to 'recruit'. My friend and I just could not think of any Catholic equivalent to this, so we had to reassure ourselves that in all likelihood no one would ever ask us about becoming a Catholic. Nevertheless, the question, along with an impression of Evangelical Christians, has stayed with me.

At about the same time my friend and I were having our conversation, Pope John Paul II was beginning to enunciate a concept – the so-called "new evangelisation" – which was aimed primarily at those who had lost an active sense of the Catholic faith but who had not, in many cases, abandoned all religious allegiance or sensibility. The unstated assumption in the conversation my friend and I were having was that the questioner was not a Catholic and never had been. Strictly speaking, this distinguished him or her from the principal target groups of the new evangelisation. However, if we had been more reflective we would have realised that there was another important dimension to our discussion about welcoming people into the Church. Some elementary calculations would have revealed a telling point. The university we were attending had well over 20,000 students. Assuming the enrolment reflected national trends, we could estimate that about 5,000 students were Catholic. But our Catholic student club had no more than 30 active members. We could have easily asked ourselves at least two additional questions. First, why were so few Catholics joining the club, assuming that wanting to join a Catholic student group was a sign of wanting to deepen religious commitment? Second (and a development of our actual discussion), if an 'inactive' Catholic came to us wanting to reanimate his or her faith, what we would suggest?

For many decades there has been a sense in the Catholic community that this lack of strong religious commitment will, in time, right itself. A common corollary of this view – what Argyle and Beit Hallahmi call the "traditional theory" – was that this lack of fervour would correct itself and, after a period of searching, many would re-emerge at some time in the future as engaged and committed Catholics.[2] Instead of seeing the issue of so many loosely affiliated Catholics as urgent, many argue that the glass is not half empty but half full. But there are some consequences to this view. For example, such a view can lead to a certain complacency, as if those involved in leadership and planning do not need to take action, given that what is being played out is almost a natural life history. For such a mindset, alarmist over-reaction, which does not recognise the lifecycle of faith development, is to be avoided.

More recently, in 2004, I was approached to lead a research project to examine the needs, concerns, and aspirations of Catholic university students. Funding for the project was not extravagant. Our methodology depended on being able to speak to participants who were members of functioning groups. We did not have the resources to identify students ourselves, so we planned to make contact with university Catholic student groups and ask them to assist us in contacting suitable participants. The project was never undertaken because it was very hard to find extant university Catholic student groups. Even at my *alma mater,* where the student enrolment had grown to close to 35,000, the Newman Society had been defunct for many years.[3] In the intervening decades, the vitality of Catholic university fellowship had not seemed to improve. From any number of perspectives, this is neither a reassuring nor an isolated situation.

2 Michael Argyle and Benjamin Beit-Hallahmi, *The Social Psychology of Religion.* (London: Routledge & Kegan Paul, 1975), 65.
3 An interesting aside was that many of the universities we contacted had what appeared to be vibrant and well subscribed groups catering for overseas Catholic students.

At the very least, the lack of an active university presence at many universities could be a significant portent of the future, and part of a much wider trend that needs to be both understood and addressed. This book proceeds on the hopeful basis that the mentality that surrounds discussion of such issues has changed. More than forty years after the Council, it is time to discuss responses, both pastoral and conceptual, which recognise that to admit the serious challenges facing the Church, and especially Catholic schools, is not a capitulation to an unfounded pessimism, but an acknowledgment of the present reality and of the Church's ability to respond.

1

John Paul II and the "New Evangelisation"

Introduction

The term new evangelisation came to prominence in the writings and, more generally, in the pontificate of Pope John Paul II; it can be described as the *leitmotif* of his apostolate.[1] As such, what will be discussed here is John Paul's new evangelisation. It is important to state at the outset that the new evangelisation as envisaged by Pope John Paul is a program directed to the Church at large. Catholic schools have a role to play, but this is one part of a much broader vision. In this chapter, a detailed, rigorous description and contextualisation of the origins and scope of the new evangelisation will be given. This is critical, since discussion of the new evangelisation needs to be based on a very firm understanding of what the term means.

As it becomes more widely known and used, there is some danger that it will become somewhat clichéd, a term that may cover a range of assumed meanings. Indeed, in my work I have seen quite a few examples where different peoples' conception of what the new evangelisation might mean are at odds with each other. This makes progress on a common course of action difficult because goals can be in conflict. A clear sense of the new evangelisation is particularly important in a work such as this which seeks to apply it, in a practical sense, to the future direction and configuration of Catholic schools. This first chapter, therefore, will seek to establish, at some length,

---

1 Weigel remarked, "The new evangelisation [is] the basic concept central to the pontificate of John Paul II," George Weigel, *Witness to Hope: The Biography of Pope John Paul II.* (Cliff Street Books: New York, 1999), 554. This point is reiterated in George Weigel, *The End and the Beginning: Pope John Paul II – The Victory of Freedom, the Last Years, and the Legacy.* (New York: Doubleday, 2010), 445-447.

the new evangelisation as arising from a legitimate understanding of the missionary nature of the Church, and in continuity with not just the teachings of the Second Vatican Council but the broader Catholic tradition. Situating the discussion in this context allows for some of the dimensions and implications of the new evangelisation for Catholic schools to be spelled out, although a more complex and detailed discussion of contemporary missiology and related issues is outside the scope of this book.[2]

The key reference point for the new evangelisation is the Encyclical Letter, *Redemptoris Missio* of Pope John Paul II.[3] This Encyclical can be seen in an historical continuum starting with the conciliar decree on missionary activity, *Ad Gentes,* and Pope Paul VI's apostolic exhortation, *Evangelii Nuntiandi.* In this regard, *Redemptoris Missio* provides an example of the Catholic understanding of the Tradition both as conserving the essentials of the past and as responding to new realities and challenges.[4]

For Pope John Paul II, this new phase of evangelisation was not new in the sense of being an innovation that moved beyond the Church's traditional mission of proclaiming the Gospel to all nations. Rather, a new sense of evangelisation emerged from the teachings of the Second Vatican Council, and in the social reality of many secular Western countries, such as Australia.[5] Pope John Paul II identified three elements in the Church's commitment to evangelisation. The first was the essential missionary focus of the Church on proclaiming

---

2 Louis Luzbetak, *The Church and Culture: New Perspectives in Missiological Anthropology.* (New York: Orbis, 1988).
3 John Paul II, 'Encyclical Letter, *Redemptoris Missio*', in J. Michael Miller, (Ed), *The Encyclicals of John Paul II.* (Huntington, IN; Our Sunday Visitor Inc, 1996). Hereafter referred to as "RM."
4 Avery Dulles, *The Reshaping of Catholicism: Current Challenges in the Theology of Church.* (San Francisco: Harper and Row, 1988), 75-93.
5 Dulles, *Reshaping,* 144-149.

the Gospel of Christ to those who have not heard it.[6] This remains the proper, or classical, sense of the term. The second element focused on those with strong Christian affiliation who were "fervent in their faith and Christian living."[7] However, there was a third, intermediary element, and it is from here that the new evangelisation, as treated in this book, takes its meaning.

> Particularly in countries with ancient Christian roots, and occasionally in the younger Churches as well, where entire groups of the baptised have lost a sense of the faith, or even no longer consider themselves members of the Church, and live a life far removed from Christ and his Gospel ..., in this case what is needed is a "new evangelisation" or a "re-evangelisation.[8]

Notice that here Pope John Paul II is moving beyond the traditional distinction between catechesis and evangelisation. Catechesis is directed to those who have already received the Gospel as a salvific reality. The goal of catechesis is to nurture the faith of believers and to make them better disciples of Christ. Evangelisation is primarily directed toward those who have never heard the Gospel. In launching the new evangelisation, Pope John Paul II is confident that these categories need to be modified in the context of an increasing secular culture in countries such as Australia. To be sure, many people are baptised, but they have lost a living sense of the Gospel. What is needed here is not catechesis or evangelisation in the strict sense, but a new concept, namely, the new evangelisation.

---

6 For stylistic reasons, Church is used to signify the Catholic Church unless otherwise stated.
7 RM, 33.2.
8 RM, 33.3.

From Vatican II to Pope John Paul II's New Evangelisation

Origins of the new evangelisation

Schindler has argued that the intellectual origins of the new evangelisation can be traced to John Paul II's Christocentric reading of *Gaudium et Spes*.[9] In the Pope's anthropology, each person is created in the image and likeness of God. Thus, each person has inalienable rights and an inviolable dignity.[10] The fundamental task of the Church is to promote and defend this dignity at every opportunity. Dulles described this vision as a "prophetic humanism": "The central and unifying task of the Church, for John Paul II, is to rediscover and promote the inviolable dignity of every human person."[11] Although many are immersed in cultures which do not value the transcendent, people of today cannot avoid the profound existential questions that emerge in their search for meaning and purpose.[12] Their searching is rooted in their origins as creatures of God. A sense of unease or incompleteness is part, therefore, of the very human condition. Human history can be seen as a long tale of the search by people for answers about their existence, origins, final destiny and, perhaps

---

9 Pastoral Constitution on the Church in the Modern World, *Gaudium et Spes*, in Austin Flannery (Ed), *Vatican Council II. The Sixteen Basic Documents*. (Northport, N.Y: Costello Publishing Company, 1996). David L. Schindler, 'Reorienting the Church on the Eve of the Millennium: John Paul II's New Evangelisation', *Communio*, 24 (Winter), 1997, 729-779. For a sense of how John Paul II interprets *Gaudium et Spes* (hereafter referred to as "GS"), see John Paul II, *Crossing the Threshold of Hope*. (New York: Alfred A. Knopf,1994), 48-50.
10 GS, 12. This has long been a concern of Pope John Paul II. Dziwisz remarks that John Paul's contribution to the Council was "[the] reassertion of the centrality of the person within a robust Christocentric framework," Stanislaw Dziwisz, *A Life with Karol: My Forty-Year Friendship with the Man Who Became Pope*. (New York: Doubleday, 2007), 19.
11 Avery Dulles, 'The Prophetic Humanism of John Paul II' in Avery Dulles, *Church and Society: The Laurence J. McGinley Lectures, 1988-2007*. (New York: Fordham University Press, 2008), 142-156 at 143.
12 Kenneth L. Schmitz, *At the Centre of the Human Drama: The Philosophical Anthropology of Karol Wojtyla/John Paul II*. (Washington, D.C: Catholic University of America Press, 1993); John Saward, *Christ is the Answer: The Christ-Centred Teaching of Pope John Paul II*. (Edinburgh: T&T Clark, 1993).

most urgently, a clear sense of how to live. For many, this search is unfulfilled, and no more so than in the past few centuries when human questioning has often been resolved in violent and contradictory ideologies.

For Pope John Paul II, these existential and unavoidable questions find their ultimate resolution in an encounter with the living Christ, who is preeminently experienced in communion with the Church. In *Gaudium et Spes*, this is expressed as Christ uniting himself in some way with every human being.[13] The presence of Christ thus reaches into every aspect of human culture because of the divine identity of each person. To evangelise, then, is not to impose something on human beings; rather, evangelisation seeks to address a profound human need, to provide something that is lacking but which is sorely needed. One of the tasks of the Church is to proclaim this message in many situations where culture is seen in far more positivistic terms, and where discussion of God is pushed to the margins of public discourse.[14]

In its witness to Christ, the Church has a cultural role of synthesis in its effort to relate Christian faith to particular cultures. Nevertheless, a genuine synthesis has yet to be achieved. Indeed, in many places, the dominant cultural forces push people further away from the Gospel.[15] This is particularly the case in many Western, developed countries (their ancient Christian traditions notwithstanding), and in countries such as Australia, despite a period of unprecedented missionary growth in previous centuries. In order to make Christ known, the Church – which is missionary by its very nature – must adopt a new posture with innovative strategies and approaches in response to a changed cultural context. In this new approach, responsibility for

13 GS, 22.
14 GS, 56.
15 John Paul II, 'Apostolic Constitution *Ex Corde Ecclesiae*', *Origins*, 20, October 4, 1990, 273.

evangelisation is broadened, not to devalue the role of priests and religious, but to include the whole ecclesial community. Hence, the laity has a critical role in the new evangelisation.[16] The Pope's renewed emphasis on the evangelising role of the laity builds on Vatican II's teaching on the mission of the laity as it is expressed in the document, *Apostolicam Actuositatem.*[17]

The new evangelisation and the laity

The contribution of the laity was further promoted in the Apostolic Exhortation of 1988, *Christifideles Laici.*[18] This document spelled out the role of the laity as integral to the missionary activity of the Church.[19] The involvement of the laity in "temporal affairs and earthly activities" – and it is hard to think of a better example of this than those who work in Catholic schools – is essential if the Church is to fulfill its role as a leaven in society.[20] To illustrate this point, the scriptural image of "labourers in the vineyard" was used to underline the obligation of all the People of God, not just the clergy and professed religious, to proclaim the Kingdom.[21] The unity of the Church as a communion of individual believers comes from their communion with Christ: "From the communion that Christians experience in Christ there immediately flows the communion which they experience with one another: all are branches of a single vine,

16 Giovanni Magnani, 'Does the So-Called Theology of the Laity Possess a Theological Status?' in Rene Latourelle, (Ed), *Vatican II Assessment and Perspectives: Twenty-Five Years After (1962-1987).* Volume One. (New York: Paulist Press, 1988), 569-633.
17 Decree on the Apostolate of Lay People, *Apostolicam Actuostatem,* in Flannery, *Vatican Council II,* 5.
18 Peter V. Hai, 'A Study of John Paul II's Theology of the Laity in Ecclesia in Asia with Reference to the Documents of the Federation of Asian Bishop's Conferences', *Australian Journal of Theology,* 2007, Pentecost Edition.
19 John Paul II, Apostolic Exhortation, *Christifideles Laici* (hereafter referred to as "CL"). (Homebush, NSW: St Paul Publications, 1988).
20 CL, 15-17.
21 CL, 2.

namely, Christ."[22] The ecclesial identity of the laity was underlined by Pope John Paul II when he stressed that being part of this communion was both a gift and a task for lay people, one which directs them to a closer union with God.[23] This idea recalls the great conciliar theme, spelt out most clearly in *Lumen Gentium*, where all are called to holiness, which is an inner conversion marked by a strong personal relationship with Christ.[24] With their communal life centred in Christ, all members of the Church act in the unity of the Holy Spirit in their outreach to the world. *Christifideles Laici* clearly related the common responsibility for mission to an authentic ecclesial existence. The imperative of evangelisation flows from membership in the Church, where all share St. Paul's sense of the critical nature of their vocation: "Woe to me if I do not preach the Gospel."[25] The centrality of evangelisation is a manifestation of a radical way of life. Hai has pointed out that the call to holiness and to witness as used by Pope John Paul II can be equated with what is called in other magisterial documents, "the perfection of charity."[26]

Emerging social conditions add critical urgency to the evangelising responsibility of the laity. In Australia, and many other countries, the numbers of those in ordained ministry or who are professed religious, is steadily declining. In addition, the connection of many people, including Catholics, to the Church through parish networks is becoming far more tenuous. The people most likely to come into contact with those who have "lost a living sense of the Gospel" are lay people in the course of their everyday professional and personal lives. When traditional approaches are proving ineffective, new types

---

22 CL, 18.
23 CL, 20.
24 LG, 78.
25 1 Cor 9:16.
26 Hai, 'Theology of the Laity', 4, cf. CL, 16.

of lay associations with a specific evangelical focus are required.[27] This aspect of the new evangelisation is often discussed, namely, the emphasis on using new methods. Realising these new approaches is not straightforward. William Levada, for example, and of special interest to Catholic schools, called for a new catechesis to accompany the new evangelisation but did not indicate what this involved.[28] In an often reported speech to the bishops of Latin America in Haiti in 1983, John Paul II commented on current changed social conditions affecting the Church's mission, and the need to find innovative solutions to these new realities. Evangelisation needs to be renewed in at least three senses, "[in] its ardour, methods and expression."[29] For example, *Christifideles Laici* points to the new media of mass communication as one way of narrowing the gap between faith and culture.[30] Pope John Paul II also singled out World Youth Day as an example of a new method of outreach, where "the authentic values found in popular piety" are to be found.[31]

The importance of Ad Gentes

In his writings on the new evangelisation, John Paul II made frequent reference to two documents. The first was the decree of the Second Vatican Council on the Church's Missionary Activity, *Ad Gentes*.[32] His extensive use of this decree established continuity between the teaching of the Council and his own thought: "On the one hand we can rediscover, and, as it were, read the magisterium of the last Council

---

27 Avery Dulles, 'John Paul II and the New Evangelisation', *America*, 1993, 166(3), 23-29.
28 William J. Levada, 'New Evangelisation Requires a New Catechesis', *L'Osservatore Romano*, 1998, 1543, January 7, 11.
29 John Paul II, 'The Task of the Latin American bishops', *Origins* 12, 1983, March 24, 659-662.
30 CL, 44.
31 John Paul II, *Threshold*, 115-117, at 115.
32 'Decree on the Church's Missionary Activity, *Ad Gentes*', (hereafter referred to as "AG") in Flannery, *Vatican Council II*, 2-5.

in the whole previous magisterium of the Church, while on the other
we can rediscover and re-read the whole preceding magisterial in that
last Council."[33] Michael Miller has noted that a characteristic feature
of John Paul II's encyclicals is the manner in which he embedded
the teaching of the Second Vatican Council in his own writing. To
illustrate this, he noted that in the twelve encyclicals written prior
to 1996, John Paul II made over 170 references to *Lumen Gentium*
and about 130 to *Gaudium et Spes*.[34] The theological orientation of *Ad
Gentes* draws heavily on *Lumen Gentium* in that it sees the Church as a
sacrament.[35] Based on this sacramental ecclesiology, the first chapter
of *Ad Gentes* establishes a doctrinal focus for the whole document,
and parallels the missionary life and activity of the Church with the
Trinitarian life of God. Just as the life of the Trinity is understood as
a dynamic movement, the Son and the Spirit being sent by the Father
into the world, so the Church looks beyond itself and sends out its
members to bring the salvation of Christ to all.[36]

The central concern of *Redemptoris Missio*, establishing the
permanent validity of the Church's missionary mandate, is thus seen
as a legitimate development of conciliar teaching, since the Council
did not envisage any decrease in missionary fervour in the post-
conciliar period.[37] Indeed, in a speech made prior to the Council, Pope
John XXIII remarked: "The purpose of the Council is, therefore,
evangelisation."[38] In *Ad Gentes*, missionary evangelisation is seen as

33 John Paul II, *Sources of Renewal, The Implementation of Vatican II.* (San Francisco: Ignatius
Press, 1994), 40.
34 J. Michael Miller (Ed), *The Encyclicals of John Paul II.* (Huntington, IN: Our Sunday
Visitor Press, 1996), 29.
35 AG, 1.
36 AG, 3.
37 Carl, E. Braaten, 'A Papal Letter on the Church's Missionary Mandate', *Dialog*, 30,
182-183, 1991. Timothy O'Donnell, 'The Crises of Faith and the Theology of Mission:
A Reflection on Redemptoris Missio', *Faith and Reason*, 18(3), 5-13, 1992.
38 Quoted in Giuseppe Alberigo and Joseph A. Komonchak, *History of Vatican II.*
(Maryknoll, NY: Orbis, 1995), vol 1, 439.

an essential manifestation of ecclesial life, a point made explicit in the opening sentence of the document: "The Church on earth is by its very nature missionary."[39] In *Ad Gentes,* evangelisation is never seen as being tangential to the life of the Church; it is always an area of perennial importance.[40] It cannot then be properly described as an activity undertaken by a small number of specialists but, rather, should be something that marks, to some degree, all the people of God. *Ad Gentes* maintains, nonetheless, the traditional conception of Christian mission as an outreach to "two billion people – and their number is increasing day by day – who have never, or barely, heard the Gospel message."[41] Seeing the agents of evangelisation in wider terms opens up the possibility of viewing mission not as something only directed to the "mission lands" of the third world, but as an activity which can be carried out wherever Christians find themselves.[42] As most Christians are not clerics or part of religious congregations that have a particular missionary focus, one of the principal means of evangelisation is the witness given by Christians in the conduct of their daily lives. This implicit broadening of the concept of the missionary agent is an important antecedent for the new evangelisation, aimed as it is at regions that have a Christian heritage.

> For all Christians, wherever they live, are bound to show forth, by the example of their lives and by the witness of the word, that new

39 AG, 2. *The New Dictionary of Theology* notes that in recent times the discussion of mission has been closely connected with evangelisation and "a distinction between the two is often seen as formal and arbitrary," *The New Dictionary of Theology,* Joseph A. Komonchak, Mary Collins, Dermot A. Lane, (Eds). (Wilmington, DE: Michael Glazier Inc, 1987), 664-668.

40 Suso Brechter, 'Decree on the Church's Missionary Activity', in Herbert Vorgrimler, (Ed), *Commentary on the Documents of Vatican II.* (Montreal: Palm Publishers, 1987), Vol IV, 87-183.

41 AG, 10.

42 William R. Burrows, 'Decree on the Church's Missionary Activity' in Timothy E. O'Connell (Ed), *Vatican II and its Documents: An American Reappraisal.* (Wilmington, Delaware: Michael Glazier, 1986), 180-197.

man put on at baptism and that power of the Holy Spirit by which they have been strengthened at Confirmation. Thus other men, observing their good works, can glorify the Father.[43]

The importance of Evangelii Nuntiandi

The second document quoted extensively in *Redemptoris Missio* is the Apostolic Exhortation, *Evangelii Nuntiandi* of Pope Paul VI, which was written in 1975, after the third general assembly of the Synod of Bishops on evangelisation.[44] This is regarded as one of the major documents of the pontificate.[45] Paul VI set out a number of themes, which reappeared in the writings of Pope John Paul II on the new evangelisation. Indeed, John Paul II acknowledged that the foundation of the new evangelisation can be found in *Evangelii Nuntiandi*.[46] The document identifies a group of countries in the Western world to which new evangelisation is addressed, namely, "a very large number of baptised people who for the most part have not formally renounced their baptism but who are indifferent to it."[47] Evangelisation is seen as central to the Church's mission and identity, and is a task that brings with it new challenges in contemporary culture:

> We wish to confirm once more that the task of evangelising all people constitutes the essential mission of the Church. It is a task and mission which the vast and profound changes of present day society make all the more urgent. Evangelising is in fact the grace

---

43 AG, 11.

44 Paul VI, Apostolic Exhortation, On Evangelisation in the Modern World, *Evangelii Nuntiandi* (hereafter referred to as "EN"). (Washington DC: United States Catholic Conference, 1975).

45 Hebblethwaite, Paul VI's biographer, made the following comment about the document: "*Evangelii Nuntiandi*, his last and finest apostolic exhortation…it is a work of discernment and synthesis." Peter Hebblethwaite, *Paul VI, the First Modern Pope*. (New York: HarperCollins, 1993), 651.

46 John Paul II, Apostolic Letter *Tertio Millennio Adveniente* (hereafter referred to as "TMA"). Obtained 5/6/2008 from, http://www.vatican.va/holy_father/john_paul_ii/apost_letters/documents/hf_jp-ii_apl_10111994_tertio-millennio-adveniente_en.html, 21.

47 EN, 56.

and vocation proper to the Church, her deepest identity. She exists
in order to evangelise.[48]

The centrality of mission is underlined in the first chapter of
the document, which is entitled, "From Christ the evangeliser
to the evangelising Church." Christ is portrayed as the template
for evangelisation, the one who transforms the Church from an
evangelised to an evangelising community. An inseparable link is
thereby established between the Church, Christ and evangelisation.
By identifying the Church with the evangelising Christ, Pope Paul
VI reiterated the Trinitarian nature of mission set out in *Ad Gentes*.
He linked evangelisation with other essential actions of the Church,
such as teaching, reconciling sinners, and "perpetuating Christ's
sacrifice in the Mass, which is the memorial of his death and glorious
Resurrection."[49] Evangelisation in *Evangelii Nuntiandi* is a theological
and pastoral concept rich with ecclesial and missiological connotations.
It is at the heart of the Church's identity and mission.

Pope Paul VI identified a range of qualities that characterised
the evangelising Church.[50] A predominant feature is a clear and
unambiguous proclamation of Jesus as Lord.[51] Evangelisation does
not, however, stop at this kerygmatic proclamation. It includes
dimensions of inner and ongoing transformation.[52] In this respect,
evangelisation is not restricted to a historical and temporal project.
Its horizon aspect is eschatological in that it connects the person and
the community with eternity, a transtemporal realisation, as it links
the person and the community with the world to come through a
profound personal encounter with Christ.

---

48 EN, 5.
49 EN, 4.
50 EN, 6-16.
51 EN, 22.
52 EN, 23.

Evangelisation is comprehensively person-centred in its historical and in its eschatological range. Here, Pope Paul VI, anticipating *Christifideles Laici,* appealed to the exemplary character of Jesus' own ministry. Jesus encountered people from all walks of life – thereby evoking something of the mission of the laity in the Church's mission to the world. The ecclesial vocation of the laity positions them in a world of limitless contacts often beyond the direct influence of the ordained ministry. In his concern to privilege the secular involvement of the laity, Pope Paul VI wrote: "Lay people, whose particular vocation places them in the midst of the world and in charge of the most varied temporal tasks, must for this very reason exercise a very special form of evangelisation."[53] Whilst not denying the importance of ordained ministry, or the witness of the consecrated life of religious communities, Paul VI's strong emphasis on the laity laid the foundation of the new evangelisation. Accordingly, ministry emerges as an activity that engages the whole Church, and Catholic schools have a role to play in such a ministry.[54]

Evangelii Nuntiandi shows a refined anthropological appreciation of the influence of culture. In some respects, it must be recognised that contemporary culture is driven by priorities that are contrary to the Gospel, and at odds with its values. This conflict is not a new feature in the relationship of the Church and the world. While not repudiating the openness to the world envisaged in *Gaudium et Spes* and other conciliar documents, *Evangelii Nuntiandi* introduces a cautionary note, especially given the present cultural situation, which Paul VI saw in particularly dramatic terms:

> The split between the Gospel and culture is without a doubt the
> drama of our time, just as it was of other times. Therefore every

---

53 EN, 70.
54 Robert Christian, 'Priestly Formation for a New Evangelisation', *Seminarian*, 1991, 31(Jan-Mar), 18-134.

> effort must be made to ensure a full evangelisation of culture, or,
> more correctly, of cultures. They have to be regenerated by an
> encounter with the Gospel. But this encounter will not take place
> if the Gospel is not proclaimed.[55]

Clearly, then, the proclamation of the Gospel, which is the essence of evangelisation, must appreciate the cultural context in which it is conducted. He pointed out that the Gospel is not identical with any particular culture, but it is within a certain culture that it is proclaimed and mediated.[56] A critical enculturation is needed, however, if the Gospel is to take root, or be planted again in any culture, especially in the highly secularised milieu of many contemporary societies.[57] This enculturation rests on a proclamation of the Gospel, both by word and by deed, and an understanding of how a particular culture mediates meaning, especially in relation to foundational beliefs. It is a mistake, however, to see sensitivity to culture and a strong emphasis on missionary proclamation as being in tension with each other.[58] Even a brief examination of some of contemporary cultural norms bears this out.

Philip Gibbs has pointed out that many contemporary cultures offer unique challenges that call for a new approach to evangelisation, one that straddles traditional and modern settings. This is evidenced, for example, in island communities in Oceania where the homogeneity of village life has been fragmented beyond recognition.[59] Youth and young adults move to the large cities, and live in a new cultural milieu which has more in common with the poverty of the developed world than the traditional rhythms of village life. The proclamation of the

---

55 EN, 20.
56 EN, 21, 40.
57 Philip Gibbs, 'The Transformation of Culture as New Evangelisation for the Third Millennium in Oceania', *Studia Missionalia*, 1999, 48, 327-347.
58 John Paul II, *Asia*, 5.
59 Gibbs, 'Transformation', 327-328.

Gospel to these transplanted villagers must acknowledge the different circumstances in which they live, when compared with their parents and grandparents. In countries such as Australia, the surrounding culture is not overtly hostile to religion, but can be described as being largely indifferent. The experience of sectarianism, a vital issue in the recent past, has become far less common today. Religion, especially one that results in strong commitment, is often seen as a product of a bygone era. It may retain sentimental value but has lost its power to shape culture and the lives of individuals. To engage with this culture requires a desire to dialogue, that is, to learn the voice of the culture and how this was shaped, as well as its likely trajectory. Critically, however, the Church must be able to offer something of its own in this exchange, lest the dialogue become too one-sided and passive. The essential content of evangelisation – what the Church has to offer – is both a witness to the presence of God and to the life, death and resurrection of Jesus Christ, the Son of God.

> Evangelisation will also always contain – as the foundation, centre, and at the same time, summit of its dynamism – a clear proclamation that, in Jesus Christ, the Son of God made man, who died and rose from the dead, salvation is offered to all men, as a gift of God's grace and mercy.[60]

The notion of evangelisation as expressed in *Evangelii Nuntiandi* is not only a call to personal conversion, it also sees conversion on a wider social tableau, that is, in communal terms. There is no tension between these two aspects, and they need to be seen in harmony. Personal conversion and evangelisation of culture are inextricably linked. Cultures allow individuals to develop social and other networks, and these are pivotal in assisting the transmission of meaning in both personal and communal senses. To evangelise culture, therefore, is an indispensable part of the process of individual catechesis because

---

60 EN, 26.

it recognises the importance of community in mediating meaning. This does not stop at infrequent, episodic or superficial efforts at accommodation, but must aim for a far more profound engagement with the symbols, history, meaning and values that animate the culture in question. Here, Pope Paul VI insists that enculturation cannot work "in a purely decorative way, as it were, by applying a thin veneer, but in a vital way, in depth and right to their [i.e., the cultures] very roots."[61] To evangelise a culture in its entirety does not allow the mission of the Church to be atomised into any number of individual contacts, if only for the reason that no individual existence can be abstracted either from the world of nature, or from the social setting of human life, or from the culture that moulds the meanings and values that animate society itself.[62] The critical vehicle for the evangelisation of culture remains, however, the witness and activity of individuals who have, themselves, been deeply transformed by the action of God in their lives. It is a mistake to see evangelisation of culture, merely as a prelude to individual conversion. Both occur in close unison and are dependent upon each other.

In many ways the Australian Catholic Church is an example of the "younger Churches" referred to in *Redemptoris Missio*.[63] The split between the Gospel and culture to which Pope Paul VI referred is manifestly present and, we may suspect, is continuing to widen and, thus, demands serious attention. *Evangelii Nuntiandi* calls for new experiments, if the message of the Gospel is to be heard. The "essential content, the living substance" remains what it has always been.[64] Yet

---

61 EN, 20.

62 GS, 53.

63 Pope John Paul II, Post-Synodal Apostolic Exhortation, *Ecclesia in Oceania*, 2001, 1. Obtained on 20/10/2007 from http://www.vatican.va/holy_father/john_paul_ii/ apost_exhortations/documents/hf_jp-ii_exh_20011122_ecclesia-in-oceania_en.html.

64 EN, 25. See also John Paul II, 'Opening Address, Santo Domingo', in Alfred T. Hennelly, (Ed), *Santo Domingo and Beyond*. (Maryknoll, N.Y.: Orbis Books, 1993), 41-60.

Pope Paul VI spelled out a number of "secondary elements" as means to achieve the goal.[65] These arise from the changing circumstances of both individuals and the cultures in which they live – "the unceasing interplay of the Gospel and of man's concrete life, both personal and social."[66] Most of these secondary elements, such as preaching and pastoral care, fall within the ambit of traditional approaches, while others, such as utilisation of mass media, point to new possibilities in countries that have well developed means of communication. Further ideas for innovation are sagaciously left to the practical imagination of subsequent generations, as Pope Paul VI could hardly have envisaged the vast expansion in virtual communication that has taken place in the last two decades.

Redemptoris Missio

Redemptoris Missio sets forth Pope John Paul II's explicit teaching about the new evangelisation. Published in 1990, in celebration of the twenty-fifth anniversary of *Ad Gentes, Redemptoris Missio* was John Paul II's eighth Encyclical Letter, and it stands out as a key document in his pontificate.[67] The very title, "The Mission of the Redeemer," anticipates the Pope's presentation of the mission of the Church as flowing from the mission of Jesus himself.

Church and mission

In the Encyclical, John Paul II reaffirmed the basic missionary nature of the Church as it is treated in the conciliar and in post-conciliar documents. The impulse to mission has shaped the history of the Church from its very beginnings. As Manuel Urena has pointed out,

---

65 EN, 40-48.
66 EN, 29.
67 Manuel Urena, 'The Missionary Impulse in the Church According to Redemptoris Missio', *Communio*, 1992, 19, 94-102.

one of the goals of the encyclicals is to revive the sense of mission in changed social circumstances. The Church, by its very nature, is missionary. From this flows an obligation to evangelise, not as an act of proselytisation but as one of service.[68] John Paul II saw evangelisation, in its purest form, as an encounter with the Christ described in the terms of the Nicene-Constantinople Creed.[69] In this way, the notion of the Church as missionary is, at the same time, animated by a sense of communion with Christ and communion with others in Christ. In this context, and using Acts 4:12 as a source text, John Paul II claimed, "There is salvation in no one else, for there is no other name under heaven given by mortals by which we must be saved." Thus he reiterated that Christ was the only redeemer of humanity.[70] He noted that the message of St. Paul was given in contrast to the prevailing polytheism of his day, which was marked by a multitude of rather weak and, at times, vindictive gods battling for supremacy. The Pauline God, by contrast, was compelling and powerful, and was the Word made flesh.[71]

Proclaiming Christ

There is a clear imperative for the Church today to proclaim Christ, not in the dichotomous terms of "Jesus of history" and "Christ of faith," but as the indivisible Incarnate Word.[72] As such, Christ's salvific action ensures full communion with God through the actions of the Holy Spirit. Urena commented that this understanding of Christ as the only Redeemer of humanity contrasts with what he calls "parallel salvific mediation," a view prominent in many theological circles, often in response to the issue of the eschatological situation

---

68 RM, 46.
69 RM, 4.
70 RM, 5.
71 John 1:14.
72 RM, 6.

of the multitudes who have never heard the Gospel.[73] Pope John Paul II maintains the unique status of Christ as Redeemer, but does not imply that salvation is restricted to those who believe in Christ and have entered the Church. He recognises that:

> Today, as in the past, many people do not have an opportunity to come to know or accept Gospel revelation or to enter into the Church. The social and cultural conditions in which they live do not permit this, and frequently they have been brought up in other religious traditions.[74]

There is an underlying reference here to Karl Rahner's "anonymous Christians."[75] The fate of these individuals can be conceived of in a number of ways, all of which bear on the Christological underpinnings of evangelisation. Walter Kasper noted that in Rahner's transcendental Christology, the anonymous Christian achieves salvation in a three-step process.[76] First, there is an experience in cognition and freedom of inconceivable mystery, which is at the heart of the human condition. This is followed by a "daring hope" that this mystery, if entered into, will provide human fulfillment. Finally, a meditation on this mystery leads to the "very principle of the Incarnation" as an openness to God's self-communication of the ultimate mystery. These steps, especially the third, are not taken by all. But, by opening themselves to the fullness of being human, men and women are opening themselves to the possibility of accepting the Son of Man. Kasper, however, observed one of the limitations of this Rahnerian process by pointing out that it lacks a clear connection to Christ, and runs the risk of "metaphysicising historical Christianity and cancelling by philosophical speculation the scandal of its specific reference."[77]

---

73 Urena, *Missionary Impulse*, 97.
74 RM, 10.
75 Karl Rahner, *Theological Investigations*, Vol VI. (London: Darton, Longman & Todd, 1974).
76 Walter Kasper, *Jesus the Christ*. (New York: Paulist Press, 1976), 49-51.
77 Kasper, *Christ*, 50.

The specific reference here is the life and atoning death of Christ, which is the essence of the Church's missionary proclamation and self-identity.

Another way of looking at the eschatological dimension of those who do not believe in Christ and who have not entered the Church, is to re-evaluate the scope of Christ's atoning death. This is to emphasise the unique and unrepeatable nature of Christ's death and resurrection. Rather than drawing attention away from Christ, such an understanding centralises it. As such, it underlines the intimate link between Christ and evangelisation. Urena commented that a better way of conceptualising the fate of those outside the Church is to argue that such people enter into the salvific process by God's grace achieved by the incarnation, death, and resurrection of Jesus, a principle stated in *Ad Gentes*.[78] This is reinforced in *Redemptoris Missio*, which quotes *Lumen Gentium (13)*:

> To this catholic unity of the people of God, therefore all are called, and they belong to it in various ways, whether they be Catholic faithful or others who believe in Christ or finally all people everywhere who are by the grace of God called to salvation.[79]

The possibility of parallel salvific mediation is excluded, and thus "a necessity lies upon the Church, and at the same time a sacred duty, to preach the Gospel. Hence, missionary activity today as always retains its power and necessity."[80] Evangelisation is an essential aspect of the Church's mission and, as such, never ceases. Without it, the Church cannot be understood in any theological sense.[81] The mission to evangelise is deeply inscribed into the life and activity of the Church because it overflows from the self-communicating action of

---

78 AG, 7.
79 RM, 9.
80 AG, 7.
81 Godfried Danneels, 'Evangelisation Never Ceases', *Lumen Vitae*, 1986, 41(3), 247-259.

the Trinity itself. Just as there is the Father's 'mission' or 'sending' of the Son into the world, there is the 'mission' of the Holy Spirit from both the Father and the Son to be the crowning gift of salvation. The Trinitarian life of communion is, as it were, projected and prolonged into the world of time. The Word is made flesh in the incarnation and the Holy Spirit is poured out to be the energising gift empowering the Church to bear witness to Christ. The mission of the Church is the historical manifestation of this divine mission. The People of God proclaim Christ and act in the power of the Spirit of Pentecost - as described throughout the *Acts of the Apostles* and elsewhere in Scripture.[82] In the light of its inexhaustible and continuing Trinitarian origins, the mission of the Church is never reducible to a particular human activity or explicable in sociological categories – even though, of course, the human dimensions of Christian mission remain a legitimate subject for sociological and anthropological analysis. The most profound ecclesiological issue is the divine origin of mission:

> The first beneficiary of salvation is the Church. Christ won the Church for himself at the price of his own blood and made the Church his co-worker in the salvation of the world. Indeed Christ dwells within the Church. She is his Bride. It is he who causes her to grow. He carries out his mission through her.[83]

Trinity and mission

Elaborating on the Trinitarian foundation of both ecclesial evangelisation and communion, John Paul noted that the Holy Spirit is the principal agent of mission, and the principal witness to the living Christ.[84] As Urena pointed out, a contemporary approach to evangelisation that is rooted in *Redemptoris Missio* proceeds on the basis

---

82 See for example, Acts of the Apostles: 4:20.
83 RM, 9.
84 RM, 21.

of the harmony of the Holy Spirit's activity in Jesus Christ.[85] Echoing *Gaudium et Spes,* John Paul II asserted that the Holy Spirit allows all the possibility of sharing in the Paschal mystery.[86] The harmony of the Holy Spirit and Christ is further spelt out thus:

> This is the same Spirit who was at work in the Incarnation and in the life, death and resurrection of Jesus, and who is at work in the Church. He is therefore not an alternative to Christ, nor does he fill a sort of void which is sometimes suggested as existing between Christ and the Logos. Whatever the Spirit brings about in human hearts and in the history of peoples, in cultures and religions serves as a preparation for the Gospel and can only be understood in reference to Christ, the Word who took flesh by the power of the Spirit.[87]

In the context of John Paul II's Christological understanding of mission, the heart of evangelisation is found in the proclamation of Christ the Saviour, whatever the situation might be.[88] Consequently, the goal of evangelisation is not an imposition of Christian doctrine such that it would mean merely a passive and external acceptance of orthodox teachings in faith or morals. Because this accent has compromised the Church's missionary efforts in the past, at least to some degree, John Paul II placed special emphasis on an evangelisation that derives from and leads to a personal encounter with Christ.[89] In this intimate Christological focus, John Paul II, echoing the teaching of *Evangelii Nuntiandi,* stated that evangelisation

---

85 Urena, *Missionary Impulse,* 101.
86 RM, 28, cf GS, 10, 15, 22.
87 RM, 29.
88 RM, 44, cf EN, 27, AG, 13.
89 John Paul II made frequent reference to the new evangelisation as in essence being an encounter with Christ, for example, "[new evangelisation] is not a matter of merely passing on doctrine but rather of a personal and profound meeting with the Saviour." John Paul II, 'Commissioning of Families of the Neo-Catechumenal Way', *L'Osservatore Romano,* January 14, 1991, 12.

must aim to bring about an internal conversion of heart and mind, in an authenticity built on "a complete and sincere adherence to Christ and his Gospel."[90] The critical sign of this conversion of mind and heart is the desire to communicate the Gospel of Christ to others. Authentic Christian life is oriented to mission and evangelisation.[91]

Redemptoris Missio seeks to promote "a new awareness that missionary activity is something for all Christians, for all dioceses and parishes, Church institutions and associations."[92] In this way, it is the activity, not of individuals alone, but of the whole Church. In this regard, John Paul II reiterated the importance of the laity as missionary agents. He recalled the prominence given to lay involvement as expressed in the writings of Pius XII, through to the teaching of the Second Vatican Council, and subsequent papal teachings, including his own.[93] The new evangelisation is based on the conviction that mission is the responsibility of all members of the Church. Moreover, it is not now only a matter of sending out missionaries to other lands, but also of realising the need for Christians in secularised cultures to evangelise their many fellow citizens who, despite the evangelisation that occurred in the past, are no longer animated by the Gospel. The new evangelisation does not replace previous missiological expressions of witnessing to Christ, but enlarges the understanding of mission by taking into account the new situations. Accordingly, John Paul II proposed a more flexible, creative and informed approach to missionary work, given the variety of contexts in which it operates. In light of these differences, the local ecclesial community, with its familiarity with regional conditions,

---

90 RM, 46, cf. EN, 20.
91 John Paul II, 'Address to Bishops of Southern Germany on their Ad Limina Visit', L'Osservatore Romano, December 23, 1992, 5-6.
92 RM, 2.1.
93 RM, 7.1.

bears a special responsibility for mission in the pluralistic societies of today: "Mission is seen as a community commitment, a responsibility of the local Church."[94]

Evangelisation and culture

Evangelisation must involve an engagement with culture. On this point, John Paul II extended Paul VI's approach as expressed in *Evangelii Nuntiandi*. He specified two principles, "compatibility with the Gospel and communion with the universal Church."[95] This emphasises the complementarity of mission and communion as goals underpinning an ecclesiology sensitive to the needs of the new evangelisation. Echoing Paul VI, John Paul admitted that the optimism of the past decades regarding positive engagement with wider culture may have been, to some extent, misplaced. The "new springtime" envisaged by some has not eventuated, especially in the missionary outreach to other nations.[96]

With this in mind, John Paul II set out the cultural context of mission in today's world in Section IV of *Redemptoris Missio*. The scope of missionary activity is evoked in the title of this section, "The vast horizons of the mission *Ad Gentes*." The mission is a huge theatre of activity, and much of this is still the traditional work of missionaries in foreign lands, largely in the developing world with a comparatively brief history of Christian witness. However, the scale of the mission is enlarged when one considers a new evangelisation in those regions not traditionally regarded as mission areas. As John Paul II remarked: "Even before the Council it was said that some Christian cities and countries had become mission territories; the situation has certainly

---

94 RM, 27.
95 RM, 54.1.
96 RM, 2.2.

not improved in the years since then."[97] Catholic schools, in particular, have a role to play in the evangelising mission of the Church in these areas.

New means are called for, but the essence of the mission tradition must be preserved. For example, the Pope had no intention of undermining the traditional conduct of mission work, and certainly no wish to discourage "persons who have a special vocation to be life-long missionaries *ad gentes.*"[98] Moreover, all mission work relies on an ecclesiastical mandate in that "the bishops, as shepherds of particular Churches, are ultimately responsible for evangelising efforts."[99] Now, however, the context is broadening to include those who have not heard the Gospel, those who are part of Christian communities, and those in between who have lost a living sense of the faith.[100] This "in between" or intermediary group is most clearly the focus of the new evangelisation.

Quoting Acts 17:22-31, *Redemptoris Missio* describes St. Paul addressing the Areopagus as a metaphor for reaching out to this intermediate group. On his arrival in Athens, Paul had spoken without inhibition to a learned assembly in one of the great cultural centres of the ancient world. On the basis of his communion with Christ through the Church he proclaimed Christ to an audience that was intellectually and philosophically sophisticated – perhaps not unlike the educationally privileged classes today who, though disaffected with traditional religious practices, still search for life's meaning and, therefore, are a special concern of the new evangelisation.[101]

In summary, *Redemptoris Missio* captured a number of essential

---

97 RM, 32.1.
98 RM, 32.3, 66.
99 RM, 63.
100 RM, 33.1-33.3.
101 RM, 37.4.

components of John Paul II's understanding of the new evangelisation. The new evangelisation arises out of the teaching of the Second Vatican Council and post-conciliar writings, most notably *Evangelii Nuntiandi*. The Church is missionary in an ontological not functional sense. This is based on its Trinitarian nature and is expressed in Scripture, most notably in the *Acts of the Apostles* and the Pauline epistles. At the centre of the Church's missionary identity is the proclamation of the life, death, and resurrection of Christ, the redeemer of humanity. This proclamation of Christ takes place within a variety of cultural contexts, but is never subservient to them. The new evangelisation needs to take serious account of the cultural context in which it takes place. A better understanding of culture assists in the proclamation of the Gospel, and facilitates not so much learning about Christ as an encounter with him. Because the Church is missionary, all the faithful are called to evangelise.

Developments in the Later Writings of Pope John Paul II

John Paul II continued to elaborate on the theme of the new evangelisation in his writings and addresses after the publication of *Redemptoris Missio*.[102] For example, in *Fides et Ratio*, published in 1998, he made a particularly powerful appeal to philosophers to help explain the Church's message.[103] This "Areopagus" of philosophy – of reason in its most critical and self-reflective form – is an especially vital area in the evangelisation of culture. Implicit or explicit philosophical standpoints regarding the power of reason to arrive at truth, or to

102 John Paul II, 'Address to Bishops from the Pacific, No Task is More Important in the Pacific than the New Evangelisation', *L'Osservatore Romano*, December 16, 1998, 7-8; John Paul II, 'Address to the Bishops of the Portuguese Episcopal Conference Stating the role of Fatima in the New Evangelisation', *L'Osservatore Romano*, May 20, 1991, 8; John Paul II , 'Address to Bishops from Tuscany on Ad Limina Visit about the Necessity for New Evangelisation', *L'Osservatore Romano*, February 8, 1982, 4-5.
103 John Paul II, Encyclical Letter *Fides et Ratio* (hereafter referred to as "FR"). (Homebush, NSW: St Paul Publications, 1998).

discern the truly good, are powerful forces shaping culture. These standpoints need to be critically examined and evaluated. Philosophy, especially in its traditional meaning as the "love of wisdom", has a fundamental role in any evangelisation of culture and in promoting the dignity of the human person and its flourishing.[104] On this point, and with special reference to countries that have a long-standing Christian tradition, John Paul II wrote:

> I have unstintingly recalled the pressing need for a *new evangelisation*; and I appeal now to philosophers to explore more comprehensively the dimensions of the true, the good and the beautiful to which the word of God gives access. This task becomes all the more urgent if we consider the challenges which the new millennium seems to entail, and which affect in a particular way regions and cultures which have a long-standing Christian tradition.[105]

In *Veritatis Splendor*, published in 1993, he drew attention to the de-Christianisation of society and the erosion of previously shared moral principles.[106] A fresh effort of evangelisation is a positive response to this declining moral sense. Here, he emphasised the moral dimension of the Christian proclamation of the Gospel:

> Evangelisation – and therefore the new evangelisation – also involves the proclamation and presentation of morality. Jesus himself, even as he preached the Kingdom of God and its saving love called people to faith and conversion.[107]

We see a reiteration of an important theme in the writings of John Paul II on the new evangelisation, namely, the encounter with Christ manifesting itself in practical actions. This is also tied to a

---

104 Allen H. Vigneron, *The New Evangelisation and the Teaching of Philosophy: Essays on Fides et Ratio.* (Washington, DC: Catholic University of America, 2003), 91-108.
105 FR, 103.
106 John Paul II, Encyclical Letter, *Veritatis Splendor* (hereafter referred to as "VS") in Miller, J.M., *The Encyclicals of John Paul II.* (Huntington, IN; Our Sunday Visitor Inc, 1996), 664-771(106) at 758.
107 VS, (107.1) at 760.

more proclamatory demeanour, and has implications for, amongst other things, the way in which religious education is conducted in Catholic schools. In *Veritatis Splendor,* the encounter is in terms of a proclamation and presentation of morality. In other writings, manifestations of the new evangelisation appear in other ways. While there is an intensely personal dimension in the new evangelisation, it necessarily overflows into a vigorous social commitment, as argued in *Centesimus Annus*:

> The "new evangelisation," which the modern world urgently needs and which I have emphasised many times, must include among its essential elements a proclamation of the Church's social doctrine.[108]

We see here, the close connection between evangelisation of the person and evangelisation of culture. The two are inseparably linked. One of the characteristics of the new evangelisation is that it leads to a desire to lead others to Christ and to proclaim his Kingdom. Therefore, to see the new evangelisation as a private and interior process is to misunderstand its power. The new evangelisation calls for not only a proclamation of the Church's social doctrine but also an engagement with it in a variety of tangible forms.

Evangelisation as outreach

The need to see the new evangelisation as having a strong dimension of outreach is related to how John Paul II saw contemporary culture. As noted earlier, he shared the concerns of Paul VI about the widening gulf between the Church and wider culture. For John Paul, this gulf was a critical development, since it estranges culture from Christ, the source of all life. Moving away from Christ leads to suffering and despair. When the requirements of the new evangelisation are lived out, they provide a tangible way in which Christ can be made

---

108 John Paul II, Encyclical Letter *Centissimus Annus* (hereafter referred to as "CA"). (Homebush, NSW: St. Paul Publications, 1991), 5.

manifest in wider culture, and human suffering in all its forms can be addressed. This is another reason why the Church must live out its missionary identity. This witness is needed in a world where people have forgotten about the Gospel. It is the role of all Christians to stress Christ, and especially the suffering Christ, as the heart of missionary endeavour:

> The cross of Christ must not be emptied of its power because if the cross of Christ is emptied of its power, man no longer has roots, he no longer has prospects: he is destroyed! This is the cry of the end of the 20th century. It is the cry of Rome, of Moscow, of Constantinople. It is the cry of all Christendom: of the Americas, of Africa, of Asia, of everyone. It is the cry of the new evangelisation.[109]

In summary, the new evangelisation can be expressed in a number of dimensions, all of which, however, can be traced back to an intimate and life-changing encounter with Christ. From this encounter flows the power to engage and critically shape culture. This encounter allows specialists to see their disciplines as a locus for evangelisation – for example, for philosophers to use their expertise to critically engage in a dialogue with others. The new evangelisation must have a public face, one that is seen by others. This can occur only if it is rooted in a personal and intimate union with Christ that helps to give Catholicism an evangelical sharpness manifested in a desire to spread the Gospel by proclamation and witness.

The more radical the conversion to Christ, the more intense the commitment will be to the new evangelisation reiterated in *Novo Millennio Ineunte,* which emphasised the focal reality of Christ in the life of the Church and its mission of evangelisation.[110] Here, the

---

109 John Paul II, Apostolic Letter *Orientale Lumen.* (Homebush, NSW: St. Paul Publications, 1995), 3.
110 'Apostolic Letter *Novo Millennio Ineunte* (hereafter referred to as "NMI"). (Homebush, NSW: St Paul Publications, 2000), 15.

model for conversion is St. Paul. The sign of this conversion is a desire to preach the Gospel.

> Over the years, I have often repeated the summons to the *new evangelisation*. I do so again now, especially in order to insist that we must rekindle in ourselves the impetus of the beginnings and allow ourselves to be filled with the ardour of the apostolic preaching which followed Pentecost. We must revive in ourselves the burning conviction of Paul, who cried out: "Woe to me if I do not preach the Gospel."[111]

It is worth noting that in *Novo Millennio Ineunte*, in accord with his constant Marian devotion, John Paul II invoked Mary as the "Star of the New Evangelisation."[112]

The new evangelisation is a constant theme in the writings of John Paul II. This is evidenced by explicit references to it, as well as its incorporation in other papal writings which address a wide variety of themes. A common element in all of this discourse is the notion of the new evangelisation as transformative. It radicalises the life of the Christian. From a number of starting points, the new evangelisation leads the individual into a new and deeper relationship with Christ that transforms both personal and private life. One clear manifestation of this transformation is a renewed emphasis on taking the Gospel of Christ to the public domain in whatever way best reflects the interest and expertise of the individual. The new evangelisation thus moves from a private and personal encounter with Christ to proclamation.

The Expanding Range of Reference

The new evangelisation and synodal conferences

While the phrase "the new evangelisation" has been described with specific reference to John Paul II's major writings and addresses,

---

111 NMI, 40.
112 NMI, 58.

its range of reference continues to grow in contemporary Catholic discourse. In *Tertio Millennio Adveniente*, John Paul proposed a special assembly of the synod of bishops for each of the five continents to prepare for the new millennium. At these synods, "the theme underlying them all is *evangelisation* or rather the *new evangelisation*."[113] These synods were convoked in Europe, America, Asia, Africa, and Oceania.[114] A brief comment on three of these documents will give a sense of the centrality of the new evangelisation as an analytical tool in a number of cultural contexts.

In many ways, the preeminent audience for the new evangelisation is Europe, especially Western Europe. Stanisław Dziwisz, John Paul's secretary for over forty years, remarked on the origins of the new evangelisation in John Paul's thought: "The idea came to him when he noticed – especially during trips – that there was an urgent need to reinvigorate Churches in old Christian countries. He thought this was particularly true of Europe."[115] In *Ecclesia in Europa*, written after the European Bishops' Synod in 1999, John Paul II first identified that "Jesus Christ is our hope."[116] This again underlined the indivisibility with which Christ and evangelisation are spoken of. The situation of the Church in Europe was described in terms that are widely used in

---

113 TMA, 21.

114 The new evangelisation appears in many other papal writings to ecclesial communities, perhaps no more prominently than in documents addressed to European and American audiences, Europe being, in many senses, the heart of the new evangelisation. For example *Ecclesia in Europa* contains the following direct references to the new evangelisation, 2,23,32,37,45,46,55,60,79. Pope John Paul II, Apostolic Exhortation, *Ecclesia in Europa* (hereafter referred to as "EE"), 2003. Obtained on 10/09/2007 on the Vatican website at www.vatican.va/holy_father/john_paul_exhortations/documents/ht_jp-iicxh_20030628_ecclesia in europa_en.html. For an overview of the new evangelisation in Europe see: Friedemann Walldorf, 'Toward a Missionary Theology for Europe: Conclusions from the ecumenical debate on the new evangelisation of Europe', *European Journal of Theology*, 1997, 13(1), 29-39.

115 Dziwisz, *Karol*, 159.

116 EE, 6.

the European sociology of religion, namely, loss of memory:

> I would like to mention in a particular way *the loss of Europe's Christian memory and heritage*, accompanied by a kind of practical agnosticism and religious indifference whereby many Europeans give the impression of living without spiritual roots and somewhat like heirs who have squandered a patrimony entrusted to them by history.[117]

This is the context into which the new evangelisation must enter. The consequences of this loss of memory are manifold. Some of these are described as: fear of the future, existential fragmentation, a feeling of loneliness, increased weakening of interpersonal solidarity, and perhaps most significantly, an attempt to promote a vision of man apart from God and apart from Christ.[118] The answer to these problems is a return to Christ, "our hope." This should be expressed in a variety of ways, notably through his presence in strong Christian communities and through the witness of holy men and women.[119] The document also identified the intimate connection between Christ and the Church. Jesus Christ was described as being alive in his Church.[120] This point was made strongly to counteract the view that the Church is an unnecessary mediator between God and man. Although this point was made, in different forms, at the Reformation, in the modern European context the view that the Church is an unnecessary mediator between God and man is seen as arising out of a heightened personalism that feeds off the fragmentation of culture in many European countries.

Ecclesia in Oceania was a significant document, an Apostolic Exhortation, specifically addressing the Church in Australia, New Zealand, the Pacific, and surrounding regions. The concept of new evangelisation was prominent in the document, and was first raised in

---

117 EE, 7.
118 EE, 8-10.
119 EE, 17-22.
120 EE, 22.

the following terms:

> When Christians live the life of Christ with deeper faith, their hope grows stronger and their charity more radiant. That was the goal of the Synod, and it is the goal of the new evangelisation to which the Spirit is summoning the whole Church.[121]

The goals of the Synod and those of the new evangelisation are seen as identical. The imperatives of the new evangelisation have increasingly moved to the centre of Catholic discourse. For instance, *Ecclesia in Oceania* clearly acknowledged that the missionary efforts of the Church in the past were largely the domain of missionary priests and religious. While these efforts are appreciated, what is needed now is a new kind of evangelisation: "The call to mission is addressed to every member of the Church. The whole Church is missionary, for her missionary activity ... is an essential part of her vocation."[122]

There is no distinction made as to who is to conduct this missionary work. Indeed, this work is seen as the responsibility of all the faithful in the light of the new situations affecting the life of the Church.[123] In countries such as Australia, the challenges facing the Church are especially acute. These "are experienced by all the local Churches in Oceania, but with particular force by those in societies most powerfully affected by secularisation, individualism and consumerism."[124] In these environments, however, the Church needs to be mindful of its primary evangelical focus – to proclaim Christ.[125]

---

121 Pope John Paul II, Post-Synodal Apostolic Exhortation, *Ecclesia in Oceania* (hereafter referred to as "EO"). (Homebush, NSW: St Paul Publications), 2001, 8, see also 18.
122 EO, 13.
123 Suquiia Goicoechea Angel, 'The New Evangelisation: Some Tasks and Risks of the Present', *Communio*, 1992, Winter, 19, 515-540.
124 EO, 18. Hamilton has also identified some of the issues impacting the new evangelisation in places like Australia. Andrew Hamilton, 'New Evangelisation', *Pacifica*, 1993, 6, 347-349.
125 EO, 22.

General Directory of Catechesis

Moving now to some other documents which address the new evangelisation, *The General Directory for Catechesis* was produced by the Congregation for the Clergy in 1997 as a revision of the 1971 *General Catechetical Directory*.[126] The 1997 *General Directory* sought to balance the contextualisation of catechesis in evangelisation as envisaged by *Evangelii Nuntiandi,* and the appropriation of the content of the faith as presented in the *Catechism of the Catholic Church*.[127] It appealed to the writings of Pope John Paul II in its content. As a "general" directory, it contained within its scope not only the formation of new generations of Christians, but also the activity of the Church in every region in which it had an institutional presence. In this regard, it recognised that the Church's mission needed to adapt to different cultural settings if it is to be effective.[128] The new evangelisation is integral to the process of catechesis, as John Paul II had repeatedly emphasised. The new evangelisation takes on a special urgency especially in countries under a strong secular influence:

> These concrete situations of the Christian faith call urgently on the sower to develop *a new evangelisation* especially in those Churches of long-standing Christian tradition where secularism has made greater inroads. In this new context of evangelisation, missionary proclamation and catechesis, especially of the young and of adults, is an evident priority.[129]

The *General Directory* recognised the universal call to evangelise, but it laid particular emphasis on the role of lay catechists. They do not replace priests or religious, but they do have an indispensable role as agents of the new evangelisation. A key lay group in the

---

126 Congregation for the Clergy, *General Directory for Catechesis* (hereafter referred to as "GDC"). (Homebush, NSW: St. Paul Publications, 1997).
127 GDC, 14-15.
128 GDC, 59.
129 GDC, 26.

new evangelisation, which will be discussed again later, are teachers in Catholic schools.[130] Given the complexity of missionary activity, clear distinctions related to precise roles are not always possible. Nonetheless, the *General Directory* restated the threefold distinction used in *Redemptoris Missio* to identify the targets of missionary activity.[131] The goal of new evangelisation remains, however, a profound experience of conversion and not just exterior conformity.[132] Thus, "primary proclamation and basic catechesis are priorities."[133]

> Through the power of the Holy Spirit, the Church in Oceania is preparing for a new evangelisation of peoples who today are hungering for Christ ... A new evangelisation is the first priority for the Church in Oceania.[134]

The new evangelisation and Pope Benedict XVI

Pope Benedict XVI, both before and after his election as the successor of John Paul II, has referred to the new evangelisation in a manner which indicates his familiarity with and support of his predecessor's teaching on this point.[135] The most striking example of his support of the work of his predecessor in this regard was the establishment in 2010 of a new pontifical council dedicated to the new evangelisation. In a homily to mark vespers on the feast of Sts. Peter and Paul, Benedict described the work of the new council in terms redolent with the influence of John Paul II:

---

130 GDC 226; Therese D'Orsa, 'The New Evangelisation and its Implications for Religious Educators', *Australasian Catholic Record*, 2002, 80(3), 287-305; Stephen Schenck, 'Catholic Secondary Schools and the New Evangelisation', *Living Light*, 1993, 30, 24-32.
131 GDC, 59, cf. RM, 34.2.
132 GDC, 58c, cf. RM, 33.3.
133 GDC, 58c.
134 Benedict XVI, 'Papal Message for the XXIII World Youth Day: Sydney, Australia, July 2008, *L'Osservatore Romano*, July 25, 2007, 6-8.
135 Works published prior to his election in April 2005 will be referred to by Benedict XVI's given name, Joseph Ratzinger.

> In this perspective, I have decided to create a new organism, in the
> form of pontifical council, with the specific task of promoting a
> renewed evangelisation in countries where the first proclamation
> of the faith already resounded, and where Churches are present
> of ancient foundation, but which are going through a progressive
> secularisation of society and a sort of "eclipse of the sense of
> God," which constitutes a challenge to find the appropriate means
> to propose again the perennial truth of the Gospel of Christ.[136]

As well as specific writings on the topic, the new evangelisation as
envisaged by John Paul II dovetails with the general analysis of the
Church and culture that Benedict has developed over many decades.
Indeed Benedict has described the present times as "an epoch of new
evangelisation".[137]

The most substantial treatment of new evangelisation in the
writings of Cardinal Ratzinger was in an address given in 2000 on
the occasion of the Jubilee of Catechists.[138] He began by stressing the
difficulties inherent in the new evangelisation aimed as it is at highly
secular cultures that have, in many instances, lost all reference to the
divine and transcendent in life.[139] Such an acknowledgment makes
the proclamation of the Gospel a struggle, given the indifference and
ignorance of many in regard to the Christian message. Agents of
the new evangelisation cannot expect that their labours will yield a
substantial harvest at the beginning. Ratzinger quoted an old proverb,
"Success is not one of the names of God."[140] This idea is repeated in

---

136 Pope's Homily at Vespers for Sts. Peter and Paul, 28/6/10. Obtained on 29/9/2011
from http://www.zenit.org/article-29734?l=english
137 Pope Benedict XVI Angelus Address at Castel Gandolfo, 21/9/11 obtained on
7/10/11 from http://www.catholic.org/international/international_story.php?id=42903
138 Joseph Ratzinger, 'Address to Catechists and Religion Teachers', 12 December
2000. Obtained on 12/10/2007 from Zenit News Service at www.zenit.org/article-
17125?l=english
139 Eugene F, Hernrick, 'What Challenges does the New Evangelisation Hold?', Priest,
49, April 1993, 43-48.
140 CRT, 3.

Spe Salvi where Benedict, in his second Encyclical, proposed that the Christian virtue of hope does not equate to human progress or to an unfounded optimism. Hope is not to be measured by worldly success, but needs to be seen in a more eschatological sense.[141] The course of the new evangelisation, according to Ratzinger, derives from the close connection of the evangelist to the person of Christ, through frequent prayer and a rich sacramental life. Only on this basis can the evangelist move to proclaim the Gospel as a personal witness.[142]

Benedict again referred to the "new evangelisation" in his address for World Youth Day which was held in Sydney in 2008, where he reiterated the point made in *Ecclesia in Oceania*:

> Through the power of the Holy Spirit, the Church in Oceania is preparing for a new evangelisation of peoples who today are hungering for Christ.... A new evangelisation is the first priority for the Church in Oceania.[143]

In another address, Benedict expressed his conviction in the following words: "If faith is truly the joy of having discovered truth and love, we inevitably feel the desire to transmit it, to communicate it to others. The new evangelisation to which our beloved Pope John Paul II called us passes mainly through this process."[144] Benedict likewise endorsed other dimensions of the new evangelisation as enunciated by John Paul II. In answer to a question about how to bring about the new evangelisation, Benedict's response was twofold: first, by proclaiming Christ clearly and unambiguously, and second, by

---

141 Benedict XVI, Encyclical Letter, *Spe Salvi*. Obtained 1/12/2007 from http://www.vatican.va/holy_father/benedict_xvi/Encyclicals/documents/hf_ben-xvi_enc_20071130_spe-salvi_en.html, 2007, 17-20.
142 Ratzinger, *Address to Catechists*, 4.
143 Benedict XVI, 'Papal Message for the XXIII World Youth Day: Sydney, Australia, July 2008, *L'Osservatore Romano*, July 25, 2007, 6-8.
144 Benedict XIV, 'Message to the Diocese of Rome Convention at the Basilica of St. John Lateran', *L'Osservatore Romano*, June 20, 2007.

living in an evangelical fashion.[145] In a 2006 address to diocesan clergy, Benedict recognised the three-fold distinction found in *Redemptoris Missio*, and so spoke of new evangelisation as aimed at those with "reduced" faith as opposed to the continuous evangelisation of those associated with parishes.[146]

Concluding Comments

The new evangelisation was a central theme of the pontificate of Pope John Paul II. It seems likely to remain a critical part of Catholic discourse in the future. In John Paul II's thinking, the new evangelisation is one of the clear fruits of the Council, a path that can be traced from *Ad Gentes* to *Evangelii Nuntiandi* to his own writings.

Evangelisation is an activity that is fundamental to the Church and expresses its Trinitarian nature. The evangelising Church proclaims the risen Christ and this proclamation is a task of all Christians. The role of clergy and religious is not diminished, but a new aspect of evangelical activity is the indispensable role of the laity as agents of the new evangelisation.[147] The new evangelisation recognises that the missionary outreach of the Church takes places in a variety of contexts. Catholic schools as ecclesial institutions have a role to play in this mission. In addressing the practical challenges of the new evangelisation there must be openness to new methods and processes to engage the changed societal circumstances of many countries.

---

145 Benedict XVI, 'Meeting with the Clergy of the Diocese of Belluno-Feltre and Treviso'. Obtained on 3/12/07, Vatican website at www.vatican.va/holy_father/benedictxvi/speeches/2006/august/documents/ht_ben-xvi_spe_20070724_clero-cadore_en.html.
146 Benedict XVI, 'Address to the Priests of the Diocese of Albano'. Obtained on 21/9/2007 Vatican website at www.vatican.va/holy_father/benedictxvi/speech/2006/august/documents/ht_ben-xvi_spe_20060831_sacerdoti-albano_en.html.
147 James D. Davidson, Thomas P. Walters, Bede Cisco, Katherine Meyer and Charles Zech, *Lay Ministers and their Spiritual Practices*. (Huntington: IN: Our Sunday Visitor, 2003), esp. 59-82.

The new evangelisation as envisaged by John Paul II is a demanding task. It sets as its goal much more than a passive and loose identification with Christ or with the Church. This chapter began with a series of points that sought to encapsulate the main themes of the new evangelisation as set out in *Redemptoris Missio*. These proved a suitable framework for understanding the origin, content, and implications of the new evangelisation. One way of refining these points is to conceive of the new evangelisation as revolving around two fundamental points. The first is an emphasis on an ever deepening, personal relationship with Christ; the second is a desire to bring others into communion with Christ.

Having discussed the origins and meaning of the new evangelisation the next two chapters provide analysis, both empirical and conceptual, of some of the factors that have led to a large number of Catholics retaining some kind of loose affiliation but who fall short of being animated by the spirit of the Gospel.

2

The Dawn of a New Era: Post-Conciliar Generations and the New Cultural Landscape

Introduction

This chapter provides an overview of the cultural context of the new evangelisation. It addresses what conditions have led to the need for the new evangelisation in countries such as Australia and, as such, establishes a foundation for the further discussion of the implications of the new evangelisation for Catholic schools. The chapter argues that many Catholics lack strong religious commitment. These Catholics cannot be realistically described as disciples of Jesus, and are clearly a target group for the new evangelisation as defined by *Redemptoris Missio*. The term "commitment" is used in this chapter in two ways. In theological terms, commitment implies a close relationship with Christ, both personally and through the Church, as well as a desire to evangelise others. This is in keeping with the discussion of the new evangelisation as envisaged by Pope John Paul II.

In sociological terms, commitment, following Stark and Glock, is made up of five factors: beliefs, practice, knowledge, experience, and consequences.[1] Committed members, accordingly, have strong religious beliefs, have a high level of participation in religious practices and rituals, are well networked with other like-minded people, and are prepared to devote time and other resources to their religious community. They know, and seek to know more, about their religious

---

1 Rodney Stark and Charles Y. Glock, *American Piety: The Nature of Religious Commitment.* (Berkeley: University of California Press, 1968), 14-15.

community, its history, teachings, and demands. Committed believers also have characteristic religious experiences both of a personal and communal nature. Their membership in a religious community has clear, direct, immediate, and long-lasting consequences for how they live.

Both empirical and theoretical studies that address the issue of the religious socialisation of Catholics born after the Second Vatican Council are examined in this chapter. The Council is seen as the key demarcation event in better understanding changes in socialisation. A generational approach is followed, using "Generation X" Catholics, the first post-conciliar generation, as a departure point. Recent studies of "Generation Y" are then discussed in light of the new evangelisation. The chapter argues that a crucial factor in understanding both Generation X and Generation Y Catholics is that their religious socialisation was markedly different from those who grew to maturity in the pre-conciliar and immediate post-conciliar period. One key difference is the emergence of a sense of personal spirituality that is dissociated from religious community. The dominant Catholic narrative of strong formative experience and the transition to a new religious understanding has been replaced by a new mentality, which is characterised by, among other factors, weak affiliation. The new evangelisation, if it is to be effective, needs to recognise and respond to this new mentality.

Prologue: The End of an Era

> Ours is a time that criticises and debunks the past, that teaches an ideology, that looks forward to a utopia.[2]

Any discussion of the cultural context for the new evangelisation must acknowledge from the outset the pivotal impact of the Second

---

2 Bernard Lonergan, 'Belief: Today's Issue' in William F. Ryan and Bernard J. Tyrell (Eds), *A Second Collection*. (London: Darton, Longman & Todd, 1974), 93.

Vatican Council, and especially the situation of the Council within the tradition of the Church.[3] Is the Council a radical, but nonetheless valid, departure from what preceded it? Is it a *"hermeneutic of discontinuity and rupture?"* Or should the Council be seen through the *"hermeneutic of reform [or] continuity,"* having an obvious connection with other Councils and not marking a clear break with the past?[4] As Dulles pointed out, for theologians such as Pope Benedict XVI, the only way forward for the Church is to stress the continuity thesis.[5] This recognises that for any major world religion, the past must not be seen as a burden but rather as a foundation that gives direction to the future. As Robert Wuthnow put it: "The Church must … be backward looking; it has a special mission to preserve the past, to carry on a tradition."[6]

For a generation of Catholics, the Council proved to be a seminal

---

3 William V. D'Antonio, James D. Davidson, Dean R. Hoge, and Katherine Meyer, *American Catholics: Gender, Generation and Commitment.* (New York: Alta Mira Press, 2001). This is not to say that the Council did not occur in a much wider context of religious disquiet and realignment, a theme well developed in Hugh McLeod, H. *The Religious Crisis of the 1960s.* (Oxford: Oxford University Press, 2007).

4 These terms are from Pope Benedict XVI: "On one hand, there is an interpretation [of the Council] that I would like to call hermeneutics of discontinuity and rupture. It was frequently able to find favour among mass media, and also a certain sector of modern theology. On the other hand, there is the hermeneutics of reform, of the renewal of the continuity of the single Church-subject, which the Lord has given us." Address of his Holiness Benedict XVI to the Roman Curia Offering Them his Christmas Greetings, December 22, 2005. Obtained on 10/6/2006 at http://www.vatican.va/holy_father/benedict_xvi/speeches/2005/december/documents/hf_ben_xvi_spe_20051222_roman-curia_en.html. For a sense of the antecedents of these contrasting interpretations see John O'Malley, 'Reform, Historical Consciousness and Vatican II Aggiornamento', *Theological Studies,* 1971, (32) , 573-601; Hubert Jedin, 'The Second Vatican Council', in Hubert Jedin, Konrad Repgen, and John Dolan, (Eds), *History of the Church,* Vol. X. (New York: Crossroads, 1981), 140-162; Stephen Schloesser (Ed), *Vatican II. Did Anything Happen?* (New York: Continuum, 2007).

5 Avery Dulles, 'Pope Benedict XVI: Interpreter of Vatican II', *Laurence J. McGinley Lectures,* 468-484, esp. 471.

6 Robert Wuthnow, *Christianity in the Twenty-First Century.* (New York: Oxford University Press, 1993), 48.

experience, marking a transition from one way of being a Catholic to a new understanding. For many, the suddenness of the change was disconcerting.[7] Instead of viewing the wider society with suspicion, many in the immediate post-conciliar era had a much more dynamic and positive view of the relationship between Church and State.[8] Dulles has characterised the relationship between Church and culture into three categories, which help to understand this cultural shift: confrontation, synthesis, and transformation.[9]

The post-conciliar era can be described as moving from a confrontation model, with its emphasis on the incompatibility of the culture with the Church, to a synthesis model. In this new understanding, the aim is for culture and faith to blend, or at least to achieve a high degree of overlap. Adopting this more conciliatory demeanour, the Church stood ready to shape and promote the transmission of the Gospel in different contexts. Seeing wider society in this way required many Catholics to question their beliefs and practices and to try to see them in harmony with wider societal norms. This transition was often marked by a profound personal experience of change to which many individuals took years to adapt.[10] The danger with synthesis, however, is that it can too readily lead to assimilation, where the cultures of different groups begin to merge, with a consequent loss of identity, especially for the weaker, less resilient party.[11] In contrast to synthesis, the third model of the

---

7 James Forsyth, *Catholicism Revisited: A Guide for the Perplexed.* (Ottawa: Novalis, 2001), 11-15.

8 Edmund Campion, *Rockchoppers: Growing Up Catholic in Australia.* (Victoria: Penguin, 1982), 14-27; Ken Dryden, *The Moved and the Shaken.* (New York: Viking, 1993), 101-103.

9 Dulles, *Reshaping,* 34-50. Dulles acknowledges that this characterization is based on a condensation of Niebuhr's five-fold model.

10 Richard M. Rymarz, 'Constructing the Future: A Reflection on the Post-Conciliar Generations', *The Australasian Catholic Record,* 1999, (1), 24-33.

11 Dean Hoge, 'Interpreting Change in American Catholicism: The River and the Floodgate', *Review of Religious Research,* 1986, 27, (4), 289-299.

relationship between the Church and the wider culture is more active and interventionist. The transformative model seeks not just to acknowledge the wider culture but also to transform it in Christ.

Expectations of the Council

Prior to the Council there was a sense that the Church was in a position of strength, and the strong allegiance of many Catholics in many countries would endure and be passed on to future generations in a relatively unchallenged way.[12] In his opening address on October 11, 1962, Pope John XXIII set the tone for many, for the gathering and what was to follow: "The Council now beginning rises in the Church like daybreak, a forerunner of most splendid light. It is now only dawn."[13] Some have commented that, as a result, the Council proceeded on an optimistic assumption about what the future held for the interaction between the Catholic Church and the wider culture, suggesting more of a harmonious convergence.[14] The idea that the culture of the Church and the secular culture would achieve more of a synthesis in the post-conciliar era has not yet been realised, certainly not in Europe and in countries such as Australia, Canada and New Zealand.[15] This assumption was predicated on the culture of the Church remaining strong, cohesive, and a formative influence in

---

12 Wilde proposes that many bishops at the Council were swept up in a euphoria that had connotations of both Turner's *communitas* – an overwhelming sense of community – and Durkheim's collective effervescence – where people feel as if they have been swept up into a different world. Melissa J. Wilde, *Vatican II: A Sociological Analysis of Religious Change.* (Princeton NJ: Princeton University Press, 2007), 24.
13 Pope John XXIII, *The Documents of Vatican II*, Walter M. Abbott (Ed). (London: Geoffrey Chapman, 1966), 703-704 (Appendix).
14 Gilles Routhier, 'Finishing the Work', in Giuseppe Alberigo and Joseph A. Komonchak, (Eds), *History of Vatican II, Vol 5*, (Netherlands: Peeters Publishers, 2005), 49-143.
15 Joseph Ratzinger, *Turning Point for Europe: The Church in the Modern World-Assessment and Forecast.* (San Francisco: Ignatius Press, 1994), 145-170; Charles Fensham, *Emerging from the Dark Age Ahead: The Future of the North American Church.* (Toronto: Novalis, 2008).

the lives of younger Catholics.[16] It was not anticipated at the Council, for instance, that in the subsequent decades the Church would face the challenge of maintaining a strong Catholic identity in institutions which, in the past, had been synonymous with Catholic presence, evangelisation, and outreach.

Two examples of this challenge are provided and illustrate its scope. Wilson Miscamble argued that the Catholic identity of the University of Notre Dame, perhaps America's most prominent Catholic university, was being imperilled by the absence of committed Catholics among its faculty.[17] In a response to this concern, John McGreevy pointed out that the difficulty that Notre Dame and other Catholic universities had was that there were insufficient numbers of Catholic scholars in general in the academy.[18] He quoted a 2006 Harvard University study of the top fifty research universities in the United States which showed that only six percent of tenured or tenure-track scholars in the arts, science, or business self-identify as Catholic.[19] In terms of human resources, therefore, for Catholic universities who wish to employ committed Catholic faculty the pool is very low.

It is fair to speculate that those at the Council would not have anticipated these challenges facing even the most prestigious Catholic institutes of higher learning. In a similar vein, Carlin and

---

16 Austin Cooper, 'Vatican II – The Context', *The Australasian Catholic Record*, 2003, 80(3), 334-342, at 342. Avery Dulles, 'Vatican II: Substantive Teaching: A Reply to John O'Malley and Others', *America*, March 31 2003, 14-17, at 15.

17 Wilson D. Miscamble, 'The Faculty Problem: How can Catholic Identity be Preserved', *America*, September 10 2007, 26-28. A similar problem exists in Canada. See 'University Leadership in Short Supply', *Western Catholic Reporter*, November 3, 2008, 3.

18 Christian Smith, 'Secularizing American Higher Education: The Case of Early American Sociology' in Christian Smith (Ed), *The Secular Revolution*. (Berkeley: University of California Press, 2003), 97-159.

19 John T. McGreevy, 'Catholic Enough? Religious Identity at Notre Dame', *Commonweal*, September 28, 2007, 7-8.

his colleagues reported on a shortage of suitable applicants applying for principalships in Catholic schools across Australia, although there is no shortage of teachers who wish to work in the system and support the ethos of the schools. On the basis of their research, they proposed that one of the reasons for the reluctance of senior teachers and others to apply for principalships is that these positions require a far greater commitment to overtly Catholic principles. There is not actual opposition to these principles, but comparatively few are prepared to strongly and publicly identify with them.[20] At the time of the Council, the majority of teachers and principals in Catholic schools were professed religious.[21] It may have been hard to predict that this situation would change so radically in the following decades to a point where finding suitable, committed Catholic school leaders would present substantial difficulties.

This prologue is not intended to be a wistful looking back at the past. Although outside the scope of this book, a discussion of some of the reasons for the sudden demise of what seemed to be a resilient and cohesive Catholic culture would centre on the nature and deficiencies of the culture itself. The point of this discussion, however, is to propose that the Council marked the end of an era, and with it a mentality characterised, as it was for many, by a formative and enduring socialisation into a faith tradition. The change was both sudden and unexpected and, as a result, very difficult to anticipate and respond to. The assumption that there would always be a large, captive audience of Catholics ready to respond has proved unfounded. The new era is premised on a different assumption, namely, that the

---

20 Paul Carlin, Tony d'Arbon, Jeff Dorman, Patrick Duignan, and Helga Neidhart, *The VSAT project – Leadership Succession for Catholic Schools in Victoria, South Australia and Tasmania.* (Australian Catholic University, 2003).
21 Maurice Ryan, *Foundations of Religious Education in Catholic Schools: An Australian Perspective.* (NSW: Social Science Press, Wentworth Falls, 1997), 9-23.

Church must work much harder at gaining and retaining allegiance. In some ways, after a protracted hiatus, the new evangelisation can be seen as a response to this cultural shift, and perhaps the first sign of the promised new dawn.

Generation X Catholics: The Lost Generation

> We must admit to a period after the Council when the communication of the faith to a newer generation lost its way. A generation of young people emerged from that period – now parents of a newer generation – who "fell between the cracks". My experience as the Professor of Theology at Australian Catholic University (1994-1998) taught me a great deal about the profundity of content and the pedagogical skills that are nowadays used in the process of communicating the faith. However, we have lost a generation, and they are not to be found working at their Bibles, or attending seminars and sessions that are now increasingly difficult to run successfully. The task of recapturing the interest and enthusiasm of the present generation of young people demands extraordinary dedication and considerable skill.[22]

This discussion of the cultural context for the new evangelisation begins by examining so-called *Generation X* Catholics. Social commentators have coined the term Generation X to describe those born between approximately 1960 and 1975.[23] The precise chronological boundaries of Generation X are difficult to define and

---

22 Francis Moloney, 'Vatican II: The Word in the Catholic Tradition', *The Mix*, May 2002. Obtained on 14/6/2002 from: www.catalyst-for-renewal.com.au. D'Antonio and his colleagues express a similar sentiment in an American context: "Even if we avoid such comparisons with older generations and focus just on today's young adults, the evidence suggests that young adults are only loosely tethered to the Church," D'Antonio et al., *American Catholics Gender*, 83.

23 That is, the population cohort that followed the *Baby Boomers*. The term Generation X was popularised by the Canadian novelist Douglas Coupland. See, for example, his novel, *Generation X. (*New York: St Martin's Press, 1991).

not of critical importance.[24] The characteristics of Generation X are the subject of sizeable literature and this discussion is not intended as a thorough review. Rather, it seeks to raise a number of issues that are pertinent to a discussion of the new evangelisation.[25]

The disengagement of Generation X

The new evangelisation recognises that many Catholics maintain some form of loose affiliation with the community of faith. A critical point, therefore, in gaining a better sense of the religious disposition of Generation X Catholics is to look for measures that are indicative of higher levels of commitment. A critical indicator is participation in the sacraments, especially the Eucharist.[26] Pope Benedict XVI put the Eucharist's historical significance for early Christians in these terms:

> The Sunday Eucharist was not a commandment, but an inner necessity. Without him who sustains our lives, life itself is empty. To do without or to betray this focus would deprive life of its very foundation, would take away its inner dignity and beauty.[27]

In terms of its own self-definition, the Church describes the Eucharist as extremely important, "the source and summit of

---

24 D'Antonio and his colleagues use, in part, the following classification in their 2007 publication: pre-Vatican II Catholics (those born in 1940 or earlier), Vatican II Catholics (those born between 1941 and 1960), post-Vatican II Catholics (those born between 1961 and 1978), and Millennial Catholics (those born between 1979 and 1987). D'Antonio at al., *American Catholics Gender*, 7.

25 William Dunn, *The Baby Bust: A Generation Comes of Age.* (New York: American Demographic Books, 1993); William Mahedy and Janet Bernardi, *A Generation Alone: Xers Making a Place in the World.* (Illinios: Intervarsity Press, 1994).

26 Stark and Finke would describe Mass attendance as a prime example of objective religious commitment (Definition 14). It is objective in the sense that the tradition identifies this practice as important. Roger Stark and Rodney Fink, *Acts of Faith: Explaining the Human Side of Religion.* (Los Angles: University of California Press, 2000), 103.

27 Pope Benedict XVI, 'Homily Given at Saint Stephen's Cathedral, Vienna', *L'Osservatore Romano*, Monday, 10th of September 2007. See also Kasper, *Sacrament of Unity*, 18-19.

Christian life."[28] Mass attendance becomes especially critical for Catholics in contemporary culture where many religious groups lack sociological boundaries, that is, beliefs and behaviours that distinguish them from others in the wider society. For Roman Catholics, many other distinguishing practices, of which plainchant and fasting are but two examples, have effectively been lost.[29] Finally, Mass attendance is closely connected with the trajectory of religious faith. Charron notes that the first stage in the development of irredeemable religious indifference is "abandonment of regular attendance at religious services."[30]

In this context, Mass attendance takes on additional significance since it remains, perhaps uniquely, a marker of Catholic belief and practice. Using Mass attendance as an indicator, it would seem that large numbers of Australian Generation X Catholics have become disconnected from a pivotal religious practice.[31] Utilising data from the Australian National Church Life Survey, Dixon put the percentage of Generation X Catholics attending Mass on any Sunday

---

28 See Synod of Bishops XI Ordinary General Assembly, *The Eucharist: Source and Summit of the Life and Mission of the Church*. Obtained on 9/10/2007 from the Vatican website: www.vatican.va/roman_curia/synod/documents/vc_synod_doc_20040528_lineamenta-xi-assembly_en.html. See also, *The Catechism of the Catholic Church*. (Homebush, NSW: St Pauls/Libreria Editirice, 1995), 2181- 2182.
29 Andrew Greeley, *The Catholic Imagination, New Wine, Old Wineskins, and the Second Vatican Council*. (Berkeley, CA: University of California Press, 2000), 133. Eammon Duffy, 'Fasting: A Lost Rite', *Tablet*, 31 January 2004, 14–17.
30 Andre Charron, 'Les Divers Types de Distants' Nouveau Dialogue, 1975, vol. 11, quoted in Michael J. Gallagher, *Struggles of Faith*. (Dublin: Columba Press, 1990), 43.
31 Patrick McNamara, *Conscience First: Tradition Second*. (Albany: State University of New York Press, 1992), 23-45. David Voas and Steven Bruce (Research Note), 'The 2001 Census and Christian Identification in Britain', *Journal of Contemporary Religion*, 2001, 19, 23-28. James E. Curtis, Edward G. Grabb and Douglas E. Baer, 'Voluntary Association Membership in Fifteen Countries: A Comparative Analysis', *American Sociological Review*, 57, 139-152.

at around 8%.[32] Robert Dixon also pointed out that the idea that large numbers of Generation X Catholics return to Church at a later time often correlated with having children, is not supported by empirical evidence.[33]

Generation X and "Sheilaism"

The number of Generation X-ers who self-identity as Catholic is, of course, higher than the number who attend Mass on a regular basis.[34] Many seem willing to retain some connection to the Church, but are keen not to overplay it and thereby appear to be overtly religious. Many people, both adults and teenagers, already affiliated with Christian Churches do not find the association comparatively enjoyable. When asked to select sources of enjoyment, both adults and teenagers rated their religious group as last in a nine category scale.[35] Robert Kaiser noted a characteristically Italian variation on this sentiment. When asked about their religion, Romans are apt to reply, "*siamo cattolici, non fanatici*" – "We're Catholic, but we're not fanatics."[36] In terms of the definition of the new evangelisation, many Catholics have lost a sense of the communal, orthodox faith of the Church, but retain their own sense of what faith means in modern society.[37] Robert Bellah and his colleagues captured this sentiment well when they quoted the classic

---

32 This information derived from the 2006 count of Mass attendees was provided in a personal communication from Robert Dixon, Director, Bishop's Office for Pastoral Planning, November 20, 2007. The figure for 20-24 year-old Generation Y-ers is 5.5%, the lowest of any cohort.

33 R. Dixon, 'Mass Attendance Trends Amongst Australian Catholics: A Significant Challenge for the Catholic Church', *South Pacific Journal of Mission Studies*, 28(2), 2004, 133-143.

34 Michael Evans and Jonathon Keeley, *Australian Economy and Society 2002: Religion, Morality and Public Policy in International Perspective 1984-2002*. (Sydney: Federation Press, 2004), 51.

35 Reginald W. Bibby, *Unknown Gods: The Ongoing Story of Religion in Canada*. (Toronto: Stoddart, 1993), 213.

36 Robert B. Kaiser, *A Church in Search of Itself*. (New York: Alfred A. Knopf, 2006), 61.

37 Eddie Gibbs, *In Name Only: Tackling the Problem of Nominal Christianity*. (Wheaton, Ill: Bridgeport/Victor, 1994).

self-description given by "Sheila Larson", a young nurse in their study:

> I believe in God. I'm not a religious fanatic. I can't remember the
> last time I went to Church. My faith carries me a long way. It's
> Sheilaism. Just my own little voice.... It's just try to love yourself
> and be gentle with yourself. You know, I guess, take care of each
> other. I think He would want us to take care of each other.[38]

Sheila is the personification of a movement toward individualism
in religious expression. A feature of this transition is an emphasis
on morality, or what we do, and away from creedal conviction, or
what we believe.[39] On the twentieth anniversary of the publication
of the study by Bellah and his colleagues, David Yamane commented
that, "if Sheila Larson had today's language available to her during the
interview, she would surely have offered the contemporary mantra,
'I'm spiritual not religious'."[40] This sentiment is also indicative of the
resilience of the religious impulse. The relentless march of atheism
predicted by the 19th century positivists has not occurred. Rather,
when more traditional forms of religious belief and expression
become less common they often emerge in what Daniel Bell
described as new and different forms.[41] Bell based his argument on
the ideas of Talcott Parsons, who saw religion as a human universal,
as typical and normative as language. But the fact that many today see
spirituality, or something similar, as replacing religion should not fill
those concerned with the future of religious groups with confidence.
This is an indication that these groups are not meeting a basic human

---

38 Robert N. Bellah, Richard Madsen, William H. Sullivan, Ann Swindler, and Steven
M. Tipton, *Habits of the Heart: Individualism and Commitment in American Life.* (New York:
Harper Row, 1986), 221.
39 Robert Wuthnow, *After Heaven: Spirituality in America since the 1950s.* (Berkeley,
University of California Press, 1998), 87-116.
40 David Yamane, 'Symposium on the 20th Anniversary of Habits of the Heart:
Introduction, Habits of the Heart at 20', *Sociology of Religion,* 68(2), 2007, 179-187, at 183.
41 Daniel Bell, *The Cultural Contradictions of Capitalism.* (New York: Basic Books, 1976),
161-163.

need and that the connection between religion and spirituality has been loosened or even severed. When this occurs there are a number of consequences.

Generation X and spirituality

Michael Mason and his colleagues have described spirituality as one of the "master ideas in Western culture."[42] Its origins can be traced to the philosophers of Ancient Greece, where it was defined as immaterial and as giving rise to human attributes such as thought and reason. Later, when associated with Christianity, spirituality was seen as the way individual Christians lived out their beliefs. It could be contrasted with the public worship of the Church and was centred on private, interior, and personal practices such as prayer. When Teresa of Avila, for example, was described as having an intense spiritual life, this was the assumed sense of the term. In contrast, when a person was described as lacking spirituality, often this referred to a superficial, external practice of religious duties and obligations without much personal conviction.[43]

In recent times, spirituality has been used to describe a far wider range of practices and experiences.[44] Of particular interest is the sense in which Yamane used the term, contrasting it with religion. Spirituality in Yamane's sense often retains some of its original meaning, namely, being an interior and personal response, but it allows individuals almost complete freedom in what they choose to incorporate into a worldview, and demands little. Most importantly, it does not act as a transformative agent but allows individuals to retain

---

42 Michael Mason, Andrew Singleton and Ruth Webber, *The Spirit of Generation Y: Young People's Spirituality in a Changing Australia.* (Melbourne: John Garrett Publishing, 2007), 33.
43 E. James Cuskelly, *Walking the Way of Jesus: An Essay on Christian Spirituality*, (Strathfield: St. Paul's Publications, 1999), 12-16.
44 Jeremy Carrette and Richard King, *Selling Spirituality: The Silent Takeover of Religion.* (London: Routledge, 2005), 30, esp. 13-17.

a loose association with the transcendent, but on their own terms. In fact, if traditional Catholic spirituality, as exemplified by Teresa of Avila, was an intense, almost all-consuming effort to become closer to God, the new sense of the term can be seen, in contrast, as keeping God at a distance.

The idea of spirituality being disassociated from any strong connection with the divine is supported in relevant literature. Gary Bouma, for example, in his discussion of contemporary uses of spirituality, noted that in its common usage it has only a tangential reference to God as one of a variety of external references which serve as the focus of the spiritual quest.[45] The external reference can be some type of divinity, an aspect of the natural world or, more typically, a sense of the other. This type of diffuse spirituality tends to reinforce decisions already taken rather than encourage new insights and perspectives.

Rather than being seen as the practical expression of religion, spirituality in this sense can be quite remote from a particular religious tradition.[46] It may or may not involve any tangible connection to a community in terms of participation in common worship or services, or expressing belief in public communal forms. This religious expression would, to return to Sheila Larsen's language, violate "my own little voice." The spiritual domain then becomes essentially a personal and private one, without a common, external referent. Many today have a highly individualised spiritual expression, one that does not have a generalised applicability and cannot easily be related to others. But without recourse to a wellspring of religious symbol, belief, and metaphor, such spirituality runs the risk of lacking creative and

---

45 Gary Bouma, *Australian Soul: Religion and Spirituality in the 21st Century*. (Melbourne: Cambridge University Press, 2007), 7-16.
46 David Tacey, *The Spirituality Revolution: The Emergence of Contemporary Spirituality*. (New York: Brunner-Routledge, 2004).

formative power and also commonality of meaning. When Teresa of Avila wrote of her spiritual experiences it was in a language that was replete with reference to the spiritual universe of Catholicism, and this provided a ready reference point. Without this connection, spirituality arguably becomes idiosyncratic, superficial, and, in a certain sense, undisciplined.[47] It can be described as "quest spirituality."

Quest spirituality

There are a number of distinctive and, to some extent, predictive aspects of quest spirituality. First, quest spirituality does not see the traditional markers of Catholic identity, the most notable being participation in the sacraments, as being of particular and distinctive importance.[48] In this view, there are many ways in which Catholic identity can be expressed, and the fixation on any one form leads to distortion and is indicative of an earlier era.[49] The fact that so many are not regular worshippers does not seriously challenge this sense of being a Catholic. Other individually chosen indicators of religious identity, therefore, become especially important. Despite this highly personal aspect, there are a number of features of religious identity that are common to those who see contemporary religion in terms of spiritual quest. For example, religious identity is not defined by theological views but by a strong sense of moral values. These values are often seen as being indicative of a more genuine spirituality as opposed to the external piety associated with institutional religion. This leads to the second aspect of quest spirituality, namely, the

---

47 Tacey, *Spirituality Revolution*, 36-37.
48 Dean Hoge, William Dinges, Mary Johnson and Juan Gonzales, J., *Young Adult Catholics: Religion in a Culture of Choice.* (Notre Dame, Indiana: University of Notre Dame Press, 2001).
49 D'Antonio and his colleagues note that 76% of American Catholics do not see weekly Mass attendance as an important indicator of what constitutes a good Catholic, D'Antonio et al., *American Catholics Today*, 27.

making of a critical distinction between the institutional Church and a more amorphous Church, the latter being the one that claims the stronger allegiance.

The institutional Church is associated with the worshipping community, and with holding common foundational beliefs. The more amorphous Church is, by definition, hard to characterise, but makes significantly fewer demands. Related to this is the third aspect of quest spirituality, namely, that it recognises that individuals do not completely disassociate themselves from Catholicism, but remain connected on their own terms. Implicit here is a loss of strong commitment to any view, or affiliation with any organisation, and also a reluctance to completely disassociate from any view or group.[50] Fourthly, quest spirituality looks to the more active and committed allegiance of younger Catholics sometime in the future. It sees the religious journey as being marked by conflict and then by some resolution, which may include a reconnection on a more significant level with the religious tradition. As a result of this, perhaps, as a global statement of pastoral intent, quest spirituality sees younger Catholics as displaying a spiritual strength that is expressed in different ways, most commonly in a concern for others and for the wider world. Accordingly to this view, the Church needs to accompany people on their journeys and minister to them from "the side" rather than making too many demands.[51]

A key feature of contemporary culture is its ineffectiveness in imparting formative religious experiences that can establish the basis of a later exploration of spirituality within a specific context. This

---

50 Many have termed this type of religious affiliation "cafeteria Catholicism," where the individual chooses what part of the tradition they want to incorporate into their own lives. For a discussion of this term see, Graeme English, 'Cafeteria Catholics', *Catholic School Studies*, 72(2), 1999, 18-23.
51 Mason et al., *Generation Y*, 6-37.

context is not in itself the end of the search, but it does provide a strong foundation. A key contributing factor in understanding the culture in which many youth and younger adults are immersed is its lack of strong, common, formative religious experiences. Although it can only be noted here, this in turn calls into question many of the conventional models of the religious trajectory of adolescents and emerging adults. The five-fold path used by Tacey, for example, to support his argument of a spiritual resurgence among youth and young adults seems to be based on a false premise, at least as it relates to younger Catholics today. His first two stages, "1. Natal faith – I was born into a religious family, and inducted into its faith traditions; and 2. Adolescent Separation – I began to ask questions about faith in teenage life, questions for which I did not receive satisfactory or adequate answers," simply did not exist for many post-conciliar Catholics.[52] The lack of formative religious experience marks a strong distinction between generations of Catholics and needs to be further examined as one of the important conditions that have led to the need for the new evangelisation in countries such as Australia.

The Religious Socialisation of Generation X

One pivotal factor that works against high levels of religious commitment, but does not lead to an immediate and definite disassociation, is a lack of religious socialisation. Generation X-ers often lack common formative experiences in youth, in what D'Orsa and D'Orsa have described as Catholic sub-cultures.[53] In recent times, this has also marked the growth to maturity of many younger

---

52 Tacey, *Spirituality Revolution*, 107. Tacey seems to base his arguments on data that he gathered from his own students. There are serious methodological and ethical issues with this type of data gathering.
53 Therese D'Orsa and Jim D'Orsa, Grounding Hope in Uncertain Times, in Anne Benjamin and Dan Riley (Eds.). *Catholic Schools: Hope in Uncertain Times.* (Mulgrave, Vic.: John Garratt Publishing, 2008).

Catholics where the impact of religious socialisation has been greatly weakened. Marie Cornwall noted that religious socialisation is of critical importance in encouraging and maintaining religious beliefs and practices.[54] Socialisation allows the social base of religion to develop. Once this is established, individuals then know how to live in the religious world inhabited by those like them. This gives rise to a certain commonality of views. One way of viewing Generation X Catholics is to draw a distinction between them and earlier generations by focusing on their religious socialisation.[55] The point of discrimination is the Second Vatican Council (1962-1965).[56] For pre-conciliar generations of Catholics in Australia and elsewhere, the transition from childhood to adult modes of religious affiliation was marked by a number of structural processes that ensured that the transition was supported.[57] Writing about his childhood, Moloney described this era well:

> I had been brought up a practising Catholic and the social and cultural setting of my life was steady as a rock. There was no need for the Bible, as I had the Pope, the Bishop, the Priest and weekly Mass. My belief system came from the family and a Catholic schooling, reinforced by the weekly sermon, the Sacraments of the Catholic Church, and various devotions.[58]

In the 1960s, the process of religious socialisation was dramatically challenged. This needs to be seen against the backdrop of the wider cultural impact of the first post-war generations, the so-called Baby-Boomers coming of age. This impact has been encapsulated by

54 Marie Cornwall, 'The Social Bases of Religion: A Study of Factors Influencing Religious Belief and Commitment', *Review of Religious Research*, 1987, (29), 44-56.
55 Jonathon Kelley and Nan Dirk De Graaf, 'National Context, Parental Socialisation , and Religious Belief: Results from 15 Nations', *American Sociological Review*, 1997, vol. 62, 639-659.
56 Alberic Stacpoole, *Vatican II: By Those Who Were There*. (London: Chapman, 1986).
57 Karl Rahner, *Mission and Grace*, (London: Sheed and Ward, 1963), 2-17.
58 Francis J. Moloney, "To Teach the Text: The New Testament in a New Age', *Pacifica* 11, 1998, 168.

Mason, Singleton and Webber as:

> From the mid-sixties till the late seventies, the 'Baby-Boomer' generation born in the post-World War II years was coming of age. They constituted an unusually high proportion of their populations, giving them greater social influence than young people usually possess. They enjoyed a prolonged adolescence while being educated, and came into their teens and twenties in a time of peace and affluence, so were targeted by marketers who created a consumer youth culture.[59]

The coming of age of this generation had profound implications, as no longer did many societal norms and conventions support religious communities, and the impact of this was dramatic. In terms of Catholicism, Bausch describes this era as "the collapse of total Church."[60] Another way of describing this change is as a movement away from a monopolistic Catholicism, where the choices and options available to Catholics were heavily prescribed. Generation X Catholics have little knowledge of the cohesive Catholic culture of the pre-conciliar world where religious socialisation was a dominant influence.[61] As they were growing up, many of the factors that had assisted the religious socialisation of earlier generations were either no longer in place, or gravely weakened, or in contradiction with each other. As Greeley claimed, what most affected religious socialisation from a Catholic perspective was the rapidity, in historical terms, and the nature of change: "When you change something that was unchangeable for 1,500 years, you are going to create a religious crisis."[62]

---

59 Michael Mason, Andrew Singleton and Ruth Webber, *Developments in Spirituality Among Youth in Australia and in Other Western Countries*, in G. Giordan (Ed) Annual Review of Sociology 2010, 110.
60 William J. Bausch, *Catholics in Crisis? The Church Confronts Contemporary Challenges.* (Mystic, CT: Twenty-Third Publications, 1999), 155.
61 Richard M. Rymarz, 'Lost Generation: The Cultures of Generation X Catholics', *Australasian Catholic Record*, April 81(2), 2004, 144-154.
62 Andrew Greeley, 'The Failures of Vatican II after Twenty Years', *America*, 1982, February 6, 86-89.

Berger and Luckman have noted that successful socialisation is dependent on common and agreed divisions in society, where socialising agents and forces are directed to the same end.[63] In medieval times, for example, the socialisation of individuals was preconfigured at birth, with family and other institutions providing socialisation toward a common goal: "[A] knight is a knight and a peasant is a peasant, to others as well as themselves."[64] In contemporary culture, however, socialisation is a far more asymmetrical and contentious phenomenon.[65] Socialisation processes compete; and if religious socialisation is not strong enough, then individuals will be formed and socialised into other worlds. Religious socialisation is largely mediated by family, peers, and institutions.[66] In a culture where religious socialisation is strong, all three work together to provide, if not a seamless, then a harmonious process where the individual learns, in many often subtle ways, what it means to be a member of that religious group. In a seminal fashion, a religious imprint is left on the core identity of the person as he or she matures.[67] In countries such as Australia, however, religious socialisation among individuals is not strong, especially in the critically important early years when core identity is being established. Catholic schools can play a role here; but without strong and ongoing support for the home and the surrounding culture, their contribution to religious socialisation is limited.

---

63 Berger and Luckman describe this as "a high degree of symmetry between objective and subjective reality." Peter L. Berger and Thomas Luckman, *The Social Construction of Reality: A Treatise in the Sociology of Knowledge.* (Garden City, NY: Anchor Books, 1967), 163.
64 Berger and Luckman, *Social Construction,* 164.
65 Peter L. Berger, *The Sacred Canopy: Elements of a Sociological Theory of Religion.* (Garden City, NY: Anchor, 1967), 127-148, esp. 138.
66 Jordi, C. Sabe, 'The Crisis in Religious Socialisation : An Analytical Proposal', *Social Compass,* 2007, 54(1), 97-111.
67 Janice L. Templeton and Jacquelynne S. Eccles, 'The Relation Between Spiritual Development and Identity Processes', in Eugene C. Roehlkepartain, Pamela Ebstyne King, Linda Wagener and Peter L. Benson, (Eds), *The Handbook of Spiritual Development in Childhood and Adolescence.* (Thousand Oaks, CA: Sage, 2006).

Establishing identity

Phillip Hammond distinguished between individual core identity
and chosen identity. One's core identity, such as being born female
or into a particular family, cannot be chosen and tends to, endure
for life, in some form.[68] In the early stages of life, socialisation is
especially important, as it reinforces specific aspects of core identity.
Religious socialisation during this period is primarily in the family, and
augmented elsewhere, schools being a notable example. Contemporary
culture, however, places the family under various pressures, such as
how time is utilised and what choices are made from a wide array of
competing priorities, and this makes the task of religious socialisation
much harder.[69]

One way of conceptualising the contemporary family dynamic
is to see it in terms of what Ralph Linton describes as "design for
living."[70] Modern society is complex and loosely integrated and offers
no overriding cultural blueprint, but in its stead allows for a range of
alternatives. "Life design" is the pattern of life embraced by a particular
sociological group. It includes a number of determining factors but
the most important is how members of the group spend their time.
The family dynamic of many households in which Generation X
Catholics grew up made familial religious socialisation problematic.
Practices such as family prayer, for example, became quite unusual.
These practices became subject to choice rather than an integral and
necessary part of family life – as they had been previously – and, thus,
no longer contributed to the religious socialisation which, in turn,

---

68 Phillip E, Hammond, 'Religion and the Persistence of Identity.' *Journal for the Scientific
Study of Religion*, 1998, 27, 1-11.
69 Raymond H. Potvin and Douglas M. Sloane, 'Parental Control, Age, and Religious
Practice', *Review of Religious Research* 27, 1985, 3-14; Joep De Hart. 'Impact of Religious
Socialisation in the Family', *Journal of Empirical Theology*, 1990, vol. 3, 59-78.
70 Ralph Linton, *The Tree of Culture.* (New York: Knopf, 1969).

weakened the establishment of core identity in the post-conciliar era.[71] Older siblings who in the past might have acted as mentors, often chose to discontinue religious practice, leaving no example for younger brothers and sisters to follow. The establishment of core identity raises a number of issues that are outside the scope of this book. One issue, however, is the pivotal role of the family as an agent of the new evangelisation. This pertains to the irreplaceable role of the family as a socialising agent, and where core identity is established.

In addition to the family, secondary socialisation also aids in the development of core identity.[72] Secondary socialisation involves other agents such as peer groups, institutions such as schools and Churches, as well as general cultural norms and plays an important role in religious socialisation.[73] Secondary socialisation, too, was compromised as Generation X matured. An example of this was the declining authority of the great institutions of society such as government, to command respect and to be followed (albeit not unquestioningly). General cultural norms, also worked against religious socialisation as the divergence between the cultures of the Church, at least in a formal sense, and the wider culture became greater. The movement from seeing religious practice and affiliation as a necessary part of an accepted cultural identity, to seeing religious practice and affiliation as a voluntary decision is a subtle change, but one which has a profound impact. In earlier times, Christian Churches could expect society to reinforce the values and attitudes they were trying to inculcate into children and teenagers, but this is now no longer the case in many

---

71 Richard M. Rymarz and John D. Graham, 'Drifting from the Mainstream: The Religious Identity of Australian Core Catholic Youth', *International Journal of Children's Spirituality*, 2006, 11(3), 371-383. Compare this with Mason et al., *Generation Y*, 121.
72 Berger and Luckman, *Construction*, 130.
73 Marie Cornwall, 'The Influence of Three Agents of Religious Socialisation : Family, Church, and Peers', in David L. Thomas, (Ed), *The Religion and Family Connection: Social Science Perspectives*. (Provo, Utah: Religious Studies Centre, 1997), 207-231.

Western secular countries.[74]

In a culture of what Roof and McKinney have called a "new volunteerism," where individuals respond to immediate needs from particular circumstances, it is up to each social agency to provide a rationale for people to remain associated, once life circumstances change.[75] In terms of the new evangelisation, the challenge is to encourage strong commitment over time, and to one body, and not to dissipate effort.[76] As Scott Appleby pointed out, however, the centrifugal forces of modern culture make the task of religious groups in this area difficult, due largely to the hegemony of the view that no decision or belief is anything more than a personal choice, one option among many.[77] Any group that wishes to claim strong allegiance must work especially hard at overcoming this cultural tendency to retain many loose associations, with no one association being privileged.

Generation X Catholics growing up

When Generation X Catholics were growing up, many of the traditional markers of Catholic identity disappeared very quickly and were not replaced with new distinctive rituals.[78] For example, the practice of Confession, or the First Rite Reconciliation, all but disappeared, and popular expressions of piety, such as sodalities or organisations, became far less popular and visible.[79] Extenuating the

74 Bibby calls this "culturally dominant socialisation," where the culture dominates individual groups in society, Bibby, *Unknown Gods*, 288.
75 Wade Clark Roof and William McKinney, *American Mainline Religion: Its Changing Shape and Future*, (New Brunswick, N.J.: Rutgers University Press, 1987), esp. 21-67.
76 David J. O'Brien, *Public Catholicism*. (New York: Macmillan, 1989), 242-252.
77 R. Scott Appleby, 'Decline or Relocation? The Catholic Presence in Church and Society, 1950-2000', in Leslie Woodcock Tentler, (Ed), *The Church Confronts Modernity: Catholicism since 1950 in the United States, Ireland & Quebec*. (Washington, D.C.: The Catholic University of America Press, 2007), 208-238.
78 Andrew Greeley, *American Catholics Since the Council: An Unauthorized Report*. (Chicago: Thomas More Press, 1985).
79 Patrick O'Farrell, *The Catholic Church and Community: An Australian History*. (Kensington: New South Wales University Press, 1985), 173-249.

loss of identity was the emphasis upon the harmony and continuity between the culture of the Church and the wider culture. Finke and Stark have described this as a transition from a high tension model, where a group had many beliefs and practices that set them apart from its environment, to a low tension model where such differences are relatively slight.[80] A group that sees itself in opposition to others has a sure means of promoting socialisation into the group, because the surrounding culture can be seen as hostile and unwelcoming.[81] Generation X Catholics, however, were brought up in an era where denominational differences were far less important than in earlier times, and where they were no longer the "out" group – the group experiencing alienation or discrimination.[82]

The post-conciliar era also brought a sense, correct or incorrect, that much of what Catholics had believed had changed, or would change in the future. As a result of this, many Catholic beliefs, practices, and teachings were challenged in a way that was unimaginable before the Council. In such an atmosphere, it was understandable that many were reluctant to strongly proclaim a distinctive Catholic position on a range of issues. To take one example of this, speaking of the 1960s and 1970s, Piderit and Morey comment:

> Many young Catholics, who at this time were trying to figure out what it meant to be a Catholic, did not get the message that weekly Mass attendance was part of the faith and cultural package. Rather, they got the unfortunate impression that Mass and Eucharist were nice, but not necessary.[83]

---

80 Roger Finke and Rodney Stark, *The Churching of America, 1776-2005: Winners and Losers in Our Religious Economy.* (New Jersey: Rutgers University Press), 43-44.
81 Duncan MacLaren, *Mission Implausible: Restoring Credibility to the Church.* (Milton Keys, UK: Paternoster, 2004), 197.
82 Donald H. Bouma, 'Understanding Group Life: Ten Contributions of Modern Society Stand Out as Helping People Comprehend Social Roles', *American Journal of Economics and Sociology*, 1991, 50(2), 57-76.
83 John Piderit and Melanie Morey, *Renewing Parish Culture: Building for a Catholic Future.* (New York: Rowman and Littlefield, 2008), 76.

This hesitancy resulted in some legitimate confusion about what were the important parts of the Tradition and how these should be passed on, and whether strong religious socialisation was necessary. A wider theological consensus would have made the task of communicating meaning to a new generation less contentious.

The formative religious experiences of Generation X Catholics, therefore, tended to be more diffuse and idiosyncratic. A connection with the transcendent dimensions of Catholicism was often lacking. Robert Barron also used the term "lost generation" to describe those Catholics who came to maturity in this era.[84] He commented that a characteristic of this time was that "the biblical and theological tended to be replaced by the political, the sociological, and, above all, the psychological."[85] Generation X Catholics find it difficult to easily recall adolescent experiences that marked their enculturation into their religious tradition. This can be contrasted with earlier generations who had a far stronger, even if not always positive, recollection of being raised Catholic.[86] These experiences have even been translated into a literary sub-genre.[87] It is unusual, by contrast, to find accounts that depict growing up Catholic in the 1970s or later. One constant feature of this era, however, was the continued strong enrolment in Catholic schools.[88]

---

84 Robert Barron, *Bridging the Great Divide: Musings of a Post-Liberal, Post-Conservative Evangelical Catholic.* (New York: Rowman & Littlefield, 2004), 193.
85 Barron, *Bridging*, 17. Barron's discussion of Religiousness A (bland, abstract, and epic) and Religiousness B (spicy, concrete, and lyrical) is also very pertinent here, 11-21.
86 These issues are discussed further in Rymarz, *Constructing*, 27-28.
87 Two examples of this subgenre are, *The Devil's Playground*, a semi autobiographical movie by director Fred Schepisi, and Ron Blair's one act play, *The Christian Brothers.*
88 Frank Martin, 'Catholic Education in Victoria 1963–1980' in *Catholic Education in Victoria Yesterday Today and Tomorrow.* (Melbourne: Catholic Education Office, 1983) 65-98.

The Catholic school and Generation X

The Catholic school, in the absence of other formative influences, became a critical factor in the religious socialisation of Generation X Catholics. The present author has identified a number of significant points that characterised the formative experience of Generation X Catholics in schools.[89] These include an overall positive experience. Generation X Catholics do not generally report negative or hostile feelings about their time in Catholic secondary schools. There is no doubt, however, that the religious education they received lacked educational focus. Generation X Catholics have a relatively poor understanding of the content of Catholicism, and most Generation X Catholics were never presented with a strong and coherent Catholic worldview, either at home or in educational settings. This resulted in a lack of religious content knowledge, a point that has been widely discussed elsewhere.[90] Because their religious socialisation was weak, many Generation X Catholics have not developed a religious vocabulary that would allow them to feel at home with the Tradition at least in a cognitive sense. When many Generation X Catholics speak about their lives and aspirations they frequently use spiritual or non-religious language to describe themselves and their lives. They see questions about God, prayer, and spiritual flourishing under the rubric of personal autonomy. Religious socialisation, if it did occur, placed great importance on experience as opposed to direct instruction and participation in religious ritual.[91] To illustrate the point, for many

---

89 Rymarz, *Generation X,* 149-151.
90 Marcellin Flynn and Magdelana Mok, *Catholic Schools 2000: A Longitudinal Study of Year 12, Students in Catholic Schools.* (Sydney: Catholic Education Commission, 2002). John C. Cavadini, 'Ignorant Catholics: The Alarming Void in Religious Education', *Commonweal,* 131, April 2004, 22.
91 Strommen and Hardel associate strong identity with a series of ritualised practices that are part of group affiliation. Mereton P. Strommen and Richard A. Hardel, *Passing on the Faith.* (Winona, Minnesota: Saint Mary's Press, 2000).

Generation X Catholics, their dominant memory of secondary school was the retreat, a time largely given over to shared reflection, which was an emerging part of the whole school curriculum in that period.[92]

If students' expectations and experiences of Catholic schools had changed, the same could be said of teachers. By the 1970s, the teaching profile of staff in Catholic schools had radically altered.[93] By far the most significant change was the inexorable rise in the number of lay teachers. The Council encouraged the laity to see themselves as an irreplaceable part of the missionary nature of the Church.[94] This understanding emerged out of a key Pauline image of the Church as the Body of Christ, which brought with it changes in the perception of teaching as both a career in the conventional sense and a living out of a vocation.

Many schools were undergoing profound structural change, and this had an impact on teaching staff.[95] One example of this was the amalgamation of schools, often as a consequence of the virtual disappearance of teaching religious. In many instances, single sex schools merged into one co-educational facility, and control of the school shifted from a religious congregation to a central agency such as the Catholic Education Office. Class sizes, which were enormous in the 1950s by present standards, reduced significantly in the 1970s and 1980s due largely to government funding which allowed for the employment of more teachers. Among other things, this altered the student-teacher relationship and allowed for a more personal relationship that would become an important factor in the way religious education was taught.

---

92 Richard M. Rymarz, 'When I was at School', *British Journal of Religious Education*, 2001, 24(1), 20-32.
93 Frank Martin. 'Catholic Education in Victoria 1963-1980', in *Catholic Education in Victoria Yesterday Today and Tomorrow.* (Melbourne: Catholic Education Office, 1983).
94 LG, 31
95 Martin, *Catholic Education*, esp. 23-32.

In classroom religious education in the 1970s, there was a pronounced shift toward more experiential pedagogical models.[96] In many ways, the experiential approach to religious education was anticipated by the short-lived kerygmatic paradigm.[97] Crawford and Rossiter have typified this era as a movement toward religious socialisation and away from religious education, making classroom religious education "less school like" and more personal.[98] These changes placed great emphasis on the learner and his or her experience of the world. This can be contrasted with the traditional style of religious education, which relied more on didactic instruction and authoritative texts.[99] The change in religious education affected not just process but also content – that is, the material that went into the curriculum and classroom teaching. The idea that key concepts and formulas needed to be at the core of the curriculum was replaced by a more dynamic understanding of Revelation that was again rooted in the learner's existential sense of how God acted in his or her life.[100] These changes produced a great deal of confusion, which was addressed by the development of *Guidelines for Religious Education*, first in the Archdiocese of Melbourne and then elsewhere. These *Guidelines* sought to apply some rigour and system to teaching, while remaining

---

96 Graham Rossiter, 'A cognitive basis for affective learning in classroom religious education', *British Journal of Religious Education*, 1997, 4(1), 4-11. Michael Buchanan, 'Pedagogical drift: the evolution of new approaches and paradigms in religious education', *Religious Education*, 2005, 100 (1), 20-37.
97 Ryan, *Foundations*, 94-98.
98 Marisa Crawford and Graham Rossiter, *Reasons for Living: Education and Young People's Search for Meaning, Identity and Spirituality*. (Melbourne: ACER Press, 2006), 424.
99 Richard Rymarz, 'Texts, Texts! An Overview of Some Religious Education Textbooks and Other Resources used in Catholic Schools from the 1950s to the 1970s', *Journal of Religious Education*, 2003, 51(1), 50-57.
100 McDermott, J, 'Avery Cardinal Dulles, S.J.: The Man in his Times for Christ's Church', in McDermott and Gavin (Eds.), *Pope John Paul II*, 224-226.

faithful to an experiential approach to religious education.[101]

In the absence of strong communal religious socialisation, like many of their contemporaries, Generation X Catholics constructed an identity from the forms that dominated the wider culture. This resulted in a personal, private, and atomised identity.[102] For many Generation X Catholics, their socialisation was into a culture that was suspicious of authority. For them, the idea of unquestioned magisterial teaching was not even a memory, much less something to which they could give strong allegiance.[103] With this background, many Generation X Catholics developed a pattern of religious life where strong expressions of belief and practice, such as regular Mass attendance, were lacking. In their place were weaker connections characterised by attendance at Church on special occasions such as Christmas or weddings, baptisms and funerals. The predominant link to the Church for Generation X Catholics, in this analysis, is their ongoing connection with Catholic schools. As their experience of them was, on the whole, positive, many Generation X Catholics want the same experience, which was not one of religious enculturation, for their own children. Enrolments in Catholic schools remain strong in most parts of Australia, therefore, because these schools meet the needs and expectations of most parents for a much more diffuse experience.

In summary, the expression of Catholicism, in which many Generation X Catholics grew to maturity, can be described as

---

101 Terence Lovat, *What is This Thing Called R.E. A decade On?* (Australia: Social Science Press, 2002).
102 Paul R. Loeb, *Generation at the Crossroads.* (New Jersey: Rutgers University Press, 1994).
103 Therese Pirola, 'Children of Vatican II: Young Adults in the Church Today', *Australasian Catholic Record*, 1987, 74(1), 1987, 314-321; Naomi Turner, *Ways of Belonging. Stories of Catholics 1910-1990.* (Blackburn: Collins Dove, 1992).

communitarian.[104] It is characterised by weak religious socialisation. Individuals see themselves as part of a wider group, but this expression is not part of their core identity and, as a result, does not have a strong impact on the way they live. Being Catholic brings with it advantages such as being able to maintain links with key institutions such as schools, and with family of origin. In terms of the new evangelisation, many Generation X Catholics are comfortable with this level of commitment, and are averse to being seen as stridently religious.[105] To encourage higher levels of religious commitment is a difficult task. Generation X Catholics tend to reflect the views of the wider culture into which they were enculturated. Just like their peers, they do not embrace commitment or close affiliations, but insist on keeping their options open. They like to see themselves as part of a broad community, and are often uneasy in establishing boundaries between themselves and others on religious grounds. In this sense, Generation X Catholics are clearly post-conciliar, an era marked by the relative absence of sectarianism.

An Overview of Generation Y

Generational changes?

The various descriptors of Generation X apply, with perhaps greater force, to subsequent generations. The lack of religious socialisation of younger Catholics should be even more acute than for Generation X because the factors that mediate religious socialisation are even more imperilled today than they were during the childhood and adolescence of Generation X. Michael Gallagher has argued that many young adults today have ever weakening formative experiences

104 Richard M. Rymarz, 'Communitarian and Commitment Models of Religious Identity', *Journal of Religious Education,* 55(3), 54-60.
105 There is more than a strong echo here, as quoted earlier, of Sheila Larsen's, "I'm not a religious fanatic."

with religion.[106] This is a conclusion that is well supported in cross-cultural studies. Table 1 on the following page taken from Mason, Singleton and Webber's 2010 study gives a sense of religiosity of high school-aged participants in a number of Western countries.

For Catholics, this should equate to less individuals expressing high levels of commitment as a function of age.[107] One example of the direction of religious affiliation amongst Catholics has been supplied by D'Antonio and his colleagues.[108] D'Antonio *et al.* observed that a trend to less commitment and greater disaffiliation seems to becoming established. They report comparisons between generational cohorts of Catholics. The following table shows the decline in commitment to the Church amongst American Catholics. The contrast between Generation X and Generation Y and earlier generations is marked.

---

106 Michael Paul Gallagher, *Clashing Symbols: An Introduction to Faith and Culture.* (New York: Paulist Press, 1998), 110-112.

107 For a comprehensive account of the decline in a wide range of religiosity measures in age related cohorts in the USA see Pierre Hegy, *Wake Up Lazarus! On Catholic Renewal.* (Bloomington: iUniverse, 2011), chapter 1, the title of which is suggestive "inconvenient statistics".

108 D'Antonio et al., *American Catholics Today,* 38-42.

Table 1. Teenagers in Australia, Britain, Canada, US: Religious beliefs, identification practices by country (percent of age-group within country)

Selected Beliefs and Practices	Aust 13-15%	Eng/Wales 13-15%	Aust 15-19%	Can 15-19%	Aust 13-17 %	USA 13-17%
Believe in God						
No	16	26	18	16	17	3
Unsure	34	33	34	48	34	12
Yes	50	41	47	37	49	84
No religious identification	44	49	51	32	48	18
Believe in life after death	59	45	75	75	56	49
Attend Church						
Weekly	16	13	13	21	15	40
Less than Weekly	47	37	45	32	46	42
Never	37	49	42	47	39	18
Pray privately once/week or more	-	-	27	30	27	65

Sources: Australia: SGY survey (Mason, Singleton and Webber 2007: 84, 90, 96, 101); England and Wales: Values Survey (Francis 2001: 27-44, 96); Canada: Project Teen Canada 2008 (Bibby 2009: 163–187); U.S.: National Study of Youth and Religion (Smith 2005: 31–43).[109]

---

109 Mason, et al.., 'Spirituality Among Youth in Australia and in Other Western Countries', in G. Giordan (Ed) *Annual Review of Sociology* 2010. Other sources Leslie Francis 2001. (*The Values Debate: A Voice from the Pupils.* London: Woburn Press. 2001), Reginald Bibby, *The Emerging Millennials.* (Lethbridge: Project Canada Books, 2009).

Table 2. Level of commitment in demographic categories in US Catholics, 2005

Generation	High Commitment %	Medium Commitment %	Low Commitment %
Pre-Vatican II (born 1940 or earlier)	43	46	12
Vatican II (born 1941-1960)	20	68	12
Post-Vatican II (born 1961-1978) identified in this study as Gen X	17	67	16
Millennials (born between 1979-1987) Identified in this study as Gen Y	0	73	27
All Catholics	21	64	15

Given the nature of quantitative statistical analysis, the finding that no millennials reported a high level of commitment to the Church is remarkable. The analysis was based on a randomly selected sample of 875 self-identified Catholics; 9%, approximately 79 individuals, were identified as millennials, making it a relatively small sample, and thus it should be treated with some caution. Notable also in the table is the high number of Generation X and Generation Y respondents in the middle category, indicating an intermediary or "wait and see" attitude, as opposed to low commitment or stronger disaffiliation.[110] This is further evidence of Generation X and Y typically wanting to keep their options open. The table also confirms the radical change in religious belief and practice that occurred between pre-conciliar

---

110 Avril Baigent, *The Y Church Report*. (RC Diocese of Northampton, 2002), 14-15.

Catholics and the generation immediately following them.[111] This is the fundamental generation gap, since following generations, with regard to religious belief and practice, resemble each other quite closely.

The spirit of Generation Y

A further examination of younger population cohorts is necessary to assist in the Australian contextualisation of the new evangelisation. The departure point for this discussion is Australian research on 13-24 year olds (born between 1981-1994) conducted by Mason and his colleagues.[112] One of their most significant findings was that in terms of religious beliefs and practices, Generation Y are very similar to their parents (45-59 years old). This again underlines the similarities between Generations X and Y.[113] Mason and his colleagues developed a typology of Generation Y to describe major groupings of spiritual and religious expression. Half of the Generation Y cohort, 54%, did not identify as Christian. They were classified as either New Age, secular, or "other", which included non-Christian religions.[114] Of the 46% Christian, 9% were committed, 8% regular, 12% marginal, and 17% nominal.[115] The numbers of Generation Y who express membership of a particular denomination has declined.[116] Amongst Generation Y Catholics, 13% were committed, 17% regular, 25%

---

111 Gary Bouma and Michael Mason, 'Baby Boomers Downunder: The Case of Australia', in Wade C. Roof, John Carroll and David Roozen, (Eds), *The Postwar Generation and Establishment Religion: Cross-Cultural Perspectives.* (San Francisco: Westview Press, 1995), 39-53.

112 Mason et al., *Generation Y,* 131.

113 Mason et al., *Generation Y,* 134.

114 Mason et al., *Generation Y,* 69.

115 Mason et al., *Generation Y,* 141.

116 Amongst Gen Y Catholics the percentage decline is 21% in the five-year period between the 1996 and 2001 census, Mason at al., *Generation Y,* 75-76. Of the entire sample 46% of Gen Y were classified as traditional Christian, 28% secular, 17% new age and 9% other.

marginal, 26% nominal, and 18% New Age.[117]

Thirty percent of Generation Y are moving away from Christian origins.[118] This is indicative of a generational movement away from Christianity, which has become stronger as the chains of memory that bind individuals to particular traditions become looser. This finding has great significance for the underlying rationale of the new evangelisation, as it suggests that the trajectory for many, who today could be described as having lost a sense of the Gospel but who are not totally disconnected from the faith Tradition of origin, is toward, over time, complete estrangement. Reginald Bibby described this process well when he commented on intergenerational religious affiliation data:

> The adult change has not involved a movement to outright atheism so much as a movement from decisiveness about belief in God to tentative belief or increasing agnosticism. With teens we see what amounts to an ongoing intergenerational shift – from tentativeness to agnosticism, and from agnosticism to atheism.[119]

This estrangement may be accompanied by some identification with spirituality, but this should be of little comfort for Christian leaders for reasons that are discussed later. At this stage, it is enough to note that if, in the end, more and more Christians become disconnected from their Churches, it matters little if this path is smooth and imperceptible or sudden and obvious. Most in Generation Y, 51%, did believe in God, but this often did not resemble the personal Christian God. A significant proportion of Generation Y, 32%, were unsure about belief in God.[120] Moreover, the trend is away from

---

117 Mason et al., *Generation Y*, 142.
118 Mason et al., *Generation Y*, 185. This can be contrasted with Bouma's discussion of 'the rise of spirituality,' Bouma, *Australian Soul*, 61-63.
119 Reginald W. Bibby, *The Emerging Millennials: How Canada's Newest Generation is Responding to Change and Choice.* (Lethbridge, AB: Project Canada Books, 2009), 169.
120 Mason et al., *Generation Y*, 83.

commitment to a more marginal and nominal expression of Christian belief and practice. Generation Y Catholics are more likely than older generations to agree that morals are relative, although on many other measures of belief they are very similar to their parents, and content to remain within the tradition into which they were born, rather than seeking out new modes of religious expression.[121]

This confirms the view that Generation Y, like their parents, are keen to keep their options open and not to commit to any view exclusively. This represents a safe option in that it does not compel the person either to believe or not believe. To find peace and happiness, most in Generation Y turn to friendship, music, work, or study. Few turn to religious or spiritual resources, even those who have some connection with religious groups. This suggests that even when these links exist, they are not strong or directional. Generation Y tends to be highly individualistic in outlook, and at the same time is not actively searching for meaning and purpose in life. Most seem content to live in a fairly proscribed circle of friends and family, to search for happiness, and to avoid above all else forcing views on others.

Other Australian research

In other Australian research, Rymarz and Graham have specifically examined active Australian Catholic youth.[122] In this work, following the descriptors used by Fulton and his colleagues, the term "active Catholic" was defined as having two of the following three criteria: regular church attendance, regular church attendance and involvement in the parish by parent(s), and being involved in something *extra* as a result of faith commitment, such as being part of a prayer group.[123] For

---

121 Mason et al., *Generation Y*, 134.
122 Rymarz and Graham, *Drifting, 375*. Richard M. Rymarz and John D. Graham, 'Going to Church: Attitudes to Church Attendance Amongst Australian Core Catholic Youth', *Journal of Beliefs and Values*, 2005, 26 (1), 55-64.
123 Fulton et al., *Young Catholics*, 7-9.

most active Catholic youth, their links with the Church can be typically described as familial (either strong or weak). It is not something that they themselves see as important but something which arises out of a commitment by their families. They are also not well networked with other active Catholic youth.[124] Most of their friends are reflective of the wider community. Most active Catholic youth are unable to articulate their religious views well, especially those that distinguish them from other groups in the community. Active Catholic youth find it hard to have their questions answered and to identify suitable religious mentors who will assist them to make the transition to adult models of faith.

There was also clear evidence of a developing disengagement among many active Catholic youth. Many students expressed the view that in the future their level of commitment and involvement would lessen. Some, perceptively, saw this as a result of decreased familial interaction corresponding with moving free of parental expectation and influence. In this way, they were repeating the pattern of their older siblings. This was, again, not a complete disaffiliation but a movement to a more culturally acceptable position where they do not disavow their religious heritage, but where it becomes much less important and requires very little of them as individuals. Finally, the active Catholic youth had great difficulty in articulating what they believed in or what the Church taught.[125]

Souls: searching, in transition and lost

One of the largest on-going projects examining youth spirituality, led

---

124 Compare with Mason et al., *Generation Y*, 121. Mason and his colleagues discuss this figure in light of the problem of over reporting in survey work.

125 Rymarz and Graham probed understanding in two areas, the Eucharist and Jesus. See Richard M. Rymarz and John D. Graham, 'Australian Core Catholic Youth, Catholic Schools and Religious Education', *British Journal of Religious Education*, 2006, 28(1) 79-88. D'Antonio and his colleagues noted a similar problem, D'Antonio at al., *American Catholics Today*, 82.

by Christian Smith, examines the religious affiliation of American teenagers.[126] Much of this work supports the claim that many teenagers today express a form of religious affiliation that makes their beliefs and behaviours hard to distinguish from general cultural norms. In terms of connection and strong identification with their Tradition, Catholic teenagers have the second weakest affiliation just ahead of Jews, but well behind conservative Protestant groups and Mormons.[127] Most US teenagers find it extremely difficult to explain what they believe. Smith and Denton argued that many religious communities are failing rather badly in religiously engaging and educating their youth. Where engagement and education of youth by their religious communities is weak, the faith of teenagers tends to degenerate into "Moralistic Therapeutic Deism" (MTD).[128]

This belief, in essence, sees religion as a moral system which, at best, generates behaviours that benefit the individual. It is highly personal and positivistic and the notion of God is relegated, not unlike in the thought of some 18th-century philosophers, to a kind of impersonal, distant force that is part of the universe, but not in an involved or decisive way. This type of belief is a not unique to Christians, but forms the background of much current discussion of the cultural forces that shape society in many Western secular countries such as Australia.[129] In many ways, MTD is a type of default position to which most without strong counter views can easily subscribe.

MTD can also be seen as an expression of a contemporary understanding of spirituality. This is not characterised by what Mason and his colleagues described as "a conscious way of life based

---

126 Christian Smith and Melinda Lindquist Denton, *Soul Searching: The Religious and Spiritual Lives of American Teenagers*. (New York, Oxford University Press, 2005).
127 Smith and Denton, *Soul*, 23-37.
128 Smith and Denton, *Soul*, 162-170.
129 Bouma, *Australian Soul*, 1-35.

on a transcendent referent," but a far more elusive sense that lacks discriminatory power.[130] The fact that many in Generation Y have not eschewed an abstract belief in God, and in some senses are trying to live a moral life, does not tell us much about them. Spirituality for them is not something that is transformative, and influences in a profound way how the person thinks or behaves.[131] The spiritual dimension of life, at least in its original conception, is not strongly developed in Generation Y. A private, personal, and diffuse spirituality is often evident.[132] This makes few demands and can be incorporated into a variety of worldviews, Christian or otherwise.

The religious trajectory of many in Generation Y, furthermore, seems to be away from strong religious commitment. In a five-year follow up study, participants in the original Smith and Denton study were re-interviewed.[133] Here, emerging adults were the least religious group in the United States, and the most likely to explicitly move away from religious origins. In the ensuing five years, for example, the proportion of the sample group identifying as Catholic had declined from 24% to 18%. By way of comparison, the not-religious group had risen from 14% to 27%.[134] Certainly, most emerging adults see religion as having a positive effect, as a place where basic moral principles are acquired, but beyond this, religion has an increasingly minor role to play. Smith and Snell describe this as a view among many emerging adults that they have "graduated" from religion, in the sense that they have gained from it all that they need and have now moved on.[135]

This graduation from religion is part of a movement into

---

130 Mason et al., *Generation Y*, 13.
131 Smith and Denton, *Soul*, 182-185.
132 Smith and Denton, *Soul*, 201-214.
133 Christian Smith with Patricia Snell, *Souls in Transition: The Religious and Spiritual Lives of Emerging Adults.* (New York: Oxford University Press, 2009).
134 Smith and Snell, *Transition*, 114.
135 Smith and Snell, *Transition*, 286-287.

adulthood and as such is the subject of Smith and his colleagues' most recent study, the title of which is quite indicative: *Lost in Transition: The Dark Side of Emerging Adulthood.*[136] Amongst the key challenges facing younger people, they note a general disengagement with society, confused reasoning, especially on moral issues, habitual intoxication, materialistic and unrealisable life goals, and damaging sexual experiences that are soon regretted. In particular, the researchers noted that a feature of emerging adulthood is the superficial and shallow moral reasoning that many in this cohort exhibit. This is not a characteristic of young people, or due to a failing on their part, but is rather seen as a condition that the wider culture propagates. Such cultural pressure, however, leaves young people in a very vulnerable position because they are not well equipped to deal with the problems of adult life. They noted, "Emerging adults resort to a variety of explanations about what makes anything good or bad, wrong or right – many of which reflect weak thinking and provide a fragile basis upon which to build robust moral positions of thought and living."[137]

Religious knowledge

There is ample evidence that many Gen Y youth and young adults have great difficulty articulating key aspects of religious traditions. Speaking from a European perspective, Grace Davie starkly noted: "An ignorance of even the basic understandings of Christian teachings is the norm in modern Europe, especially among young people; it is not a reassuring attribute."[138] This is a problem of worldwide proportions and is certainly an issue for many Gen Y Catholics. In their extensive study of American teenagers, Smith and Denton expressed surprise

---

136 Christian Smith with Kari Christoffersen, Hilary Davidson and Patricia Snell Herzog, *Lost in Transition: The Dark Side of Emerging Adulthood* (Oxford University Press, 2011).
137 Smith et al.., *Lost in Translation*, 60.
138 Grace Davie Europe, 'The Exception That Proves the Rule', in Peter Berger, (Ed), *The Desecularisation of the World.* (Grand Rapids, Michigan: Eerdmans, 1999), 83.

at the inability of Catholic youth to articulate their religious beliefs.[139] Writing in 2001, Appleby put the problem in these terms: "No previous generation of American Catholics, it could be argued, inherited so little of the content and sensibility of the faith from their parents, as have today's youth."[140] These findings are supported in Australian research, which also indicates a low level of knowledge and comprehension of core teachings amongst Catholic youth and young adults. In a telling comment in his study, Marcellin Flynn stopped asking students question about what he calls "knowledge of the Catholic faith" because they found them so hard to answer:

> It quickly became apparent that Year 12 students were not familiar at all with the theological concepts and language used. (One student in a large high school, for example, asked the writer "who is this person Grace?").[141]

Flynn remarked that only one student out of the 5,932 surveyed correctly answered all the 24 basic religious knowledge questions.[142] While detailed reasons for this lack of understanding are not the focus here, what is relevant is that this lack of understanding affects religious plausibility.[143] In the first instance, it leads to cognitive dissonance, which is the process where a mismatch develops between a person's understandings in one area when compared to another.

---

139 Smith and Denton, *Soul*, 193-198.
140 Scott Appleby, 'Challenges Facing the American Catholic Community: Evangelising Generation X', in *Church Personnel Issues*. (Cincinnati: NACPA, 2001), September, 1.
141 Marcellin Flynn, *The Culture of Catholic Schools: A Study of Catholic Schools, 1972-1993*, (Homebush, NSW: St. Paul's Publications, 1995), 237.
142 Luke Saker, 'A Study of 1st and 2nd Year Catholic University Students' Perceptions of their Senior Religious Education Classes in Catholic Schools in Western Australia' (unpublished PhD thesis). (Edith Cowan University, Perth, Western Australia, 2004); Richard M. Rymarz, 'Talking about Jesus', *Journal of Religious Education*, 54(2), 79-84; Richard M. Rymarz and John D. Graham, 'Australian Core Catholic Youth, Catholic Schools and Religious Education', *British Journal of Religious Education*, 2006, 28(1), 79-88.
143 Diane L. Moore, *Overcoming Religious Illiteracy: A Cultural Studies Approach to the Study of Religion in Secondary Education*. (New York: Palgrave Macmillan, 2007).

If there are competing explanations, people are more likely to side with the stronger one, which is the one with which they are more familiar. If younger Catholics are not able to articulate the Tradition's position, this invariably makes it weak, implausible, and likely to be pushed aside. Articulation is especially important in areas that mark the Tradition as distinctive.[144]

If individuals cannot explain to themselves and to others what makes their religious community different from others, it seems unlikely that they will have a strong commitment to it. This has both a dogmatic and moral consequence. Rymarz and Graham pointed out that active Catholic youth have a poor understanding of Eucharistic theology.[145] Thus, when they are under pressure not to attend weekly Mass, they are much less likely to resist this because they cannot articulate, in Catholic terms, what the Mass is and why it is important.[146] In the moral sphere, why should young Catholic adults, for example, not enter into a cohabiting relationship when they do not have any cogent arguments against such a relationship? If discounting the Catholic argument happens often enough, even if this is through ignorance, then the Tradition loses all substantial authority. At most, individuals may pay it some sentimental deference, but it has lost the power to shape and direct life.[147]

To summarise this section on Generation Y, these youth are particularly challenging for those who seek to engage them in

---

144 D'Antonio et al., *American Catholics Gender*, 151.
145 Rymarz and Graham, *Core Catholic*, 183-184.
146 Huels made exactly this point in relation to Mass attendance and conviction. "There must be convincing reasons for a law or teaching or there will be no compliance.... 'The law requires mass attendance on Sundays' in itself means little or nothing to persons who are not interiorly convinced that they should be going to Church on Sunday.' John M. Huels, 'The Sunday Mass Obligation, Past and Present', *Chicago Studies*, 1990, 29, 274.
147 D'Antonio suggested that one way of reanimating the Catholic identity is to retell to young people the stories of great saints and martyrs. D'Antonio, *American Catholics Gender*, 151-152.

discussion about religion, because they like to keep their options open, and are unlikely to commit to something if they cannot see some tangible benefits arising.[148] In addition they have only a limited capacity to articulate religious ideas and concepts, a deficiency that is especially marked in the area of moral reasoning. Gen Y are aware of the range of choices that are available to them, including the option to elect to have some low level allegiance to a number of positions. D'Antonio and his colleagues have suggested that one way of regarding youth and young adults today is as shoppers or consumers.[149] This consumer analogy to describe young people and religion has also been used by Bauman and others.[150] One of the earliest uses of the concept was by John Kavanaugh.[151] The idea of the contemporary young person as a consumer rather than a seeker is gaining increasing currency, and seems to fit well with the conceptual frameworks outlined here. Mason and his colleagues expressed this as a movement from obligation to consumption.[152]

The New Catholic Mentality: A Synthesis

It has been argued in this chapter that the religious experience and expression of post-conciliar Catholics, referred to here as Generation X and Y, is different from previous generations. A useful way of synthesising the issues raised in the preceding discourse is to speak of

---

148 David Tuohy and Penny Cairns, *Youth 2K.* (Dublin: Marino Institute of Education, 2000), 48-49.
149 D'Antonio et al., *American Catholics Today*, 149-150. For a more detailed discussion of consumer culture see, David Slater, *Consumer Culture and Modernity.* (Cambridge: Polity, 1997), esp. 8-28.
150 Zygmunt Bauman, *Imitations of Postmodernity.* (London: Routledge), 222-225. Crawford and Rossiter, *Reasons for Living*, 181-192. Paul Louis Metzger, *Consuming Jesus: Beyond Race and Class Divisions in a Consumer Church.* (Grand Rapids, Michigan: William B. Eerdmans, 2007), esp. 13-39.
151 John F. Kavanaugh, *Following Christ in a Consumer Society.* (Maryknoll, NY: Orbis Books, 25th Anniversary Edition, 2006). This was first published in 1981.
152 Mason et al., *Generation Y*, 255-272.

a new Catholic mentality. Furthermore, understanding this mentality provides us with a powerful way of conceptualising how the need for the new evangelisation arose, and the challenges facing it.

Generation X and Y and those who come after them, have far more in common with each other than with the generation whose formation was shaped by the monopolistic pre-conciliar era, or the immediate period of transition after the Second Vatican Council. Many Catholics today, born well after the Council, are characterised by a number of features, one of which is a more casual, less committed type of religious affiliation. Whilst not disavowing Catholic identity completely, it is weaker than previous generations. What seems to be lacking here is a sense of strong commitment and personal conversion in many Catholics today, especially younger ones. This does not equate, in most cases, to hostility toward religion, but rather a sense that religious belief does not have a significant impact on how life is lived, or on major life-shaping choices.

Many Catholics lack an identity that makes them different or distinctive from others in the general culture. Different here does not have a moral connotation. It does not mean better, but it does refer to a clear and obvious way of living and of believing that sets apart the believer from others. One way of marking this difference is by being prepared to make significant life decisions on the basis of deeply held religious convictions. These decisions may involve some personal cost. Many younger Catholics, however, seem more content to minimise the demands that being a Catholic may place on them.

In terms of the new evangelisation, many Catholics, especially youth and younger adults, have lost a strong sense of the Gospel and of fellowship with others in Christ. A key factor in understanding the religious affiliation and commitment of Catholics today and into the future are changes in religious socialisation in the post-conciliar period. The pre-conciliar mentality, which was heavily marked by both strong religious socialisation and the impact of intense and sudden change, is no longer the dominant narrative of most Catholics. As a result, the idea that Catholics need to be shaken out of a complacency that arises from progressing through life in a relatively unreflective mode, needs to be challenged. Catholics are no longer carried along by their membership of a strong and cohesive group that facilitates their movement toward adult forms of faith expression.

Collapse of the "conveyor belt"

Metaphorically speaking the "conveyor belt" that once moved Catholics from cradle to grave has irretrievably broken down. Younger Catholics today have many more options before them, and without a strong socialised sense of religious belonging are more likely to exercise this choice than to be active in a community that does not occupy an important part of their life. One choice that many make is to retain some allegiance without ever taking this to a deep, personal, or transformative level. In terms of how Pope John Paul II conceived the new evangelisation, a profound connection with the salvific Christ is usually lacking. This is one consequence of a greatly attenuated sense of God. It is one thing to say that God exists, but quite another to enter into a relationship with the awe inspiring and personal God revealed in Scripture and elsewhere.[153]

Another feature of the new Catholic mentality as described in this chapter is recognition that the Church, at present in countries such as Australia, in a historical sense, has a much diminished capacity to influence wider culture and the lives of individuals. The days when the Church represented, if only even in popular consciousness, a

153 Baylor Institute for Studies of Religion, *American Piety in the 21ˢᵗ Century: New Insights to the Depth and Complexity of Religion in the United States.* (Waco, TX: Baylor University Press, 2004).

powerful monopoly capable of teaching with uncritical authority appears to be over.[154] It does not have unlimited resources or energy and these should be prudently directed to areas where they are most likely to be effective. An important consequence of the breakdown in communal socialisation is the recognition that, in order to nurture and sponsor religious commitment, especially at transition points in life, little can be taken for granted. Rather, the Church must be prepared to constantly evangelise. As well as being prudent this is also being true to its missionary identity. In the future, Catholic socialisation will recede even further into the background. It cannot, moreover, be recreated anymore than the world and mentality of, for example, pre-Revolutionary French Catholicism can be.

This is not to say, however, that nothing can be learned from the pre-conciliar period or that the Council marked a decisive break with Tradition. On the contrary, Catholics need to be able to feel at home in the broad expanse of their history and Tradition. This involves discernment and a clear and firm sense of the needs of today. The beacon for determining how the past should be best appropriated is the teachings of the Second Vatican Council, interpreted within a hermeneutic of continuity. If we take as the norms for interpreting the teachings of the Second Vatican Council those provided by the 1985 Synod of Bishops, a firm basis for emphasising the continuity of the Church's life and teaching is established. These norms are summarised by Dulles into six points, and the fifth of these reads: "The Council must be interpreted in continuity with the great Tradition of the Church, including earlier councils."[155] A change of

---

154 Mason and his colleagues make a similar point, Mason, *Generation Y*, 338. See also RM, 30.1.
155 Avery Dulles, 'Vatican II: The Myth and the Reality', *America*, 2003, February 24, 188. John W. O'Malley, 'Vatican II: Did Anything Happen?' in Stephen Schloesser, (Ed), *Vatican II. Did Anything Happen?* (New York: Continuum, 2007), 84.

emphasis, for example, in showing how the Council reaffirmed or renewed key teachings may be in order especially for those younger Catholics who have no experience of older mentalities.[156]

An Epilogue: A Vignette of the New Religious Landscape

A dominant discourse in contemporary Catholicism has been to draw a contrast between the pre and post-conciliar eras. There are numerous instances of this, but one example is the pedagogical approach taken with parents whose children are to receive sacraments in Catholic primary schools. The author is not aware of any published study which has systematically examined these presentations, and he relies only on personal experience. This is not intended to be an empirical argument, but it does illuminate several of the stated principles. As such, it serves as what Higgins calls a "type of micro-narrative", a brief story that is both dense and illustrative.[157]

Held in the evening, information sessions give parents a general introduction to the sacrament their child will be receiving. In the case of the sacrament of Penance, a common strategy is to contrast "Confession" before and after the Second Vatican Council. This poses at least two problems. Parents today who have children in preparing for First Communion can, for the most part, be assumed to have had little or no experience of the pre-conciliar Church. In the future, this lack of experience will only become more acute. It should be realised that all references to the Church before the Council may make an impression on older Baby Boomers or their parents, but for those typically attending information sessions in the school or parish

---

156 Avery Dulles, *The Resilient Church: The Necessity and Limits of Adaptation.* (Garden City, NY: Doubleday, 1977), esp. 17-31.
157 Stephen H. Higgins, 'The Value of Anecdotal Evidence', in Lorne Tepperman and Harley Dickinson, (Eds), *Reading Sociology: Canadian Perspectives.* (New York: Oxford University Press, 2007), 11-16, at 11.

hall, now and in the future, this is an era of receding historical interest only.

The Second Vatican Council took place approximately 50 years ago, well before today's parents of primary school children were born. To the untutored ear, moreover, talk of "Confession" before and after the Council may give the impression that a new discovery has been made and that what was done in the past has now been discarded. To an audience who may be attending under sufferance, this message may only confirm their lack of interest in exploring their religious heritage. Secondly, the religious socialisation of these parents and their children has, on the whole, been weak and this is unlikely to change in the future. Most parents will have had only a limited experience of the sacrament of Penance.[158] To contrast "Confession" before and after the Council is to completely misunderstand their reality.

In terms of the new evangelisation, in general, it may be more appropriate to proceed on the basis that those to be evangelised have only ever encountered a weak religious socialisation, one that was never challenged or quickly transformed. Whilst not discounting the importance of the tensions and changes that emerged after the Second Vatican Council, these may be an example of what this author has called "the boomer dialogues."[159] These issues have great resonance for older population cohorts, but younger generations are not part of this conversation since their formative experiences were quite different and much more diffuse, exposed as they were to the "chill winds of modernity."[160] Instead of assuming much "baggage"

158 James M. O'Toole, 'In the Court of Conscience: American Catholics and Confession', in James M. O'Toole, (Ed), *Habits of Devotion: Catholic Religious Practice in Twentieth Century America*. (Ithaca, N.Y.: Cornell University Press, 2004).
159 Rymarz, *Constructing*, 24-33, at 29.
160 Bernard Lonergan, 'Belief: Today's Issue' in William F. Ryan and Bernard J. Tyrell (Eds), *A Second Collection*. (London: Darton, Longman & Todd, 1974), 93.

on the part of parents with children in Catholic schools, for example, it may be sounder to proceed on the basis that much of what is being presented at information nights and similar events is being addressed to an audience that does not have a strong sacramental sense in either cognitive or affective dimensions. A more evangelical tone may be in order, one that highlights what the Tradition is offering.

Concluding Comments

Lack of socialisation and the currency of diffuse spirituality have important consequences. One of the most significant is that many younger Catholics do not disassociate from the Church completely. For many, the weak positive experience, whilst not cultivating strong commitment, does not close the door to a more fragile connection. All of this is indicative of what can be called a new Catholic mentality. The discussion around the new evangelisation in countries such as Australia needs to take serious account of this change in basic narrative and assumptions. The experience of transition, which was so formative of older Catholics, is no longer a dominant discourse. What has replaced it is far more ineffable, and is more easily typified by what is absent and, as such, is not reactive or hostile. Many people today, especially younger ones, are aware of the options available to them, and can be typified as consumers.

Whilst the work of evangelisation may be more difficult, it does present new opportunities for outreach, especially if religious communities are able to offer something of perceived value. Here we can return to Dulles' third categorisation of the relationship between the Church and culture to provide a way forward. If we conceive of the immediate post-conciliar period as marked by a transition from confrontation to synthesis, it may be appropriate now to move into a more transformative phase.[161] In this phase, there is reciprocity between the Church and wider culture. On the one hand, the Church is influenced by the prevailing culture and, on the other hand, the Church is able to shape culture. This is based on the Church having both something to offer and a willingness to impart this.

The new evangelisation can be interpreted on a number of levels, but as Pope John Paul II pointed out, it is in its essence a reorientation of people toward Christ. It is also a manifest living out of this commitment. Seen in these terms, this is something that the Church has to offer wider culture, a proclamation that Christ calls those who have been described here as loosely affiliated Generation Y and Generation X to communion with him. Pope John XXIII captured this notion well when he commented: "It is the Church which must take Christ to the world."[162] The commitment to do this is prescribed at least in a theoretical sense because the Church's deepest identity calls it to evangelise.

---

161 Dulles, *Reshaping*, 34-50.
162 Radio message of Pope John XXIII, 11 September 1962. Obtained on 24/9/2008 from: http://www.vatican.va/holy_father/john_xxiii/speeches/1962/documents/hf_j-xxxiii_spe_19620911_ecumenical-council_it.html.

3

The Social Context for the New Evangelisation: Three Theoretical Perspectives

Introduction

The three largely sociological perspectives presented here are not exhaustive, nor are they mutually exclusive, as the complex reality of Catholics and their engagement with the Church cannot be simply described. They do offer, nonetheless, a variety of powerful conceptual lenses for further understanding the post-conciliar generations, and propose valuable insights for contextualising the new evangelisation. Further, the discussion in this chapter establishes a theoretical platform for better understanding some of the implications of the new evangelisation for Catholic schools.

The previous chapter argued that most Generation X and Y Catholics manifest a new mentality.[1] In order to further explore the conditions that have led to the new evangelisation becoming a prominent feature of Catholic discourse, some salient ideas about changing social, religious, and cultural patterns are presented. This Chapter argues that in countries such as Australia, societal conditions as understood from a number of sociological perspectives offer explanations as to why many people now describe their religious affiliation in loose, rather than overtly negative terms. At the same time, these conditions also make strong religious commitment problematic, or in terms of the new evangelisation, made for a life that is removed, but not completely severed from the gospel. This is the social context in which Catholic schools operate, and as such, the new evangelisation can be seen as a response to this new reality.

---

1 A.M. Greeley, *The Communal Catholic: A Personal Manifesto.* (New York: Seabury, 1976).

Living in the Postmodern World

> Generation X has ample reasons to be depressed. Unwelcome, tolerated at best, cast firmly on the receiving side of socially recommended or tolerated action, treated in the best of cases as an object of benevolence, charity and pity (challenged to rub salt into the wound, as undeserved) but not of brotherly help, charged with indolence and suspected of iniquitous intentions and criminal inclinations, it has few reasons to treat 'society' as a home to which one owes loyalty and concern.[2]

An overview of Bauman's postmodernity

An approach to analysing the religiosity of post-conciliar Catholics is to use the concept of postmodernity to better understand their religious affiliation. The conception of postmodernity developed by Bauman is used as an analytical framework. Bauman provided a number of strong images, such as the harshness of living from "hand to mouth", and the "pain of being stripped of self-assurance and self-esteem", to describe the situation of Generation X.[3] A powerful feature of Bauman's analysis was that the world of Generation X is, in many instances, an unforgiving place, a world of uncertainty and of alienation. Individuals are lost and without a clear sense of purpose.[4] Postmodern life places great emphasis on the individual private sphere of life and on personal reflection, especially as it relates to adapting to ever changing social and political contexts. Individual identity is never complete, and is dismantled and reconstructed regularly, so that the angst and uncertainty of the individual is also projected into the world in which he or she lives. This has resulted in a state of flux, both on

---

2 Zygmunt Bauman, *Wasted Lives: Modernity and its Outcasts.* (Cambridge: Polity Press), 13.
3 Bauman, *Lives,* 14.
4 This echoes Coupland's sense of the term: a group with no name or identity.

a personal and communal level.[5] Bauman concurs with the cautionary notes that both Pope John Paul II and Pope Benedict XVI have made about contemporary Western culture.[6] Part of this concern is the tendency to see faith and reason as contradictory, which contributes to a sense that no unified vision on the place of men and women in the cosmos can be achieved and all that can be hoped for are fragmentary ideologies.[7] The postmodern landscape, then, is typified by a loss of belief in the "grand narrative". Individuals need to rely much more on their own resources to create meaning, and this may change many times to suit particular circumstances.[8]

It is difficult to create one's own meaning without much support from a sustaining community, and so we see the emergence of personal narratives, which lack coherence, structure, and stability. This, in turn, creates insecurity as individuals are faced with a plethora of narratives, none of which is compelling or authoritative. This results in a bewildering number of options that people cannot really comprehend. The multiplicity of choice creates uncertainty, because individuals are not naturally disposed to take such radical control, at least in a theoretical sense, of their own lives. For Bauman, one of the features of the modern world was the loss of shared, uncontested, and binding values and visions. These gave individuals a clear guide and platform in the moral, political, and religious spheres. To live

---

5 Zygmunt Bauman, *Postmodernity and its Discontents*. (New York: New York University Press, 1997), 178.

6 See Joseph Ratzinger, 'Relativism: The Central Problem for Faith Today,' *Origins*, 26, October 31, 1996, 310-317.

7 Jurgen Habermas and Joseph Ratzinger, *The Dialectics of Secularisation*. (San Francisco: Ignatius Press, 2005), 77-79.

8 Bauman, *Imitations*, 23-62. Savage and her colleagues proposed the term "midi narrative" to describe the worldview of many contemporary youth and young adults. This focuses on the being happy and having good friends. Sara Savage, Sylvia Collins, Bob Mayo and Graham Cray, *Making Sense of Generation Y: The World Views of 15-25 Year Olds*, (London: Church House), 39-89.

without a guidebook, to use Bauman's terminology, is not easy and, at the very least, undermines social cohesion.[9]

The religious meta-narrative

The variety of religious expression was, for Bauman, an important aspect of postmodernity. He argued that some religious manifestations in postmodernity, such as fundamentalism, were attractive because they freed the individual from the tyranny of constant choice, and gave them a place in a meta-narrative.[10] Without a shared vision, a person's views and sense of self may change significantly over time as one system of meaning is replaced with another. Wuthnow described a process where young adults, in the face of so many options, "tinker" with what is available to them and arrive at a personalised system of meaning, which is never stable but is always being modified and adapted.[11] This creates a sense of fluidity in today's youth and young adults, which makes them reluctant to commit to the future, whether in relationships or as part of communities.[12] The sense of temporality has direct implications for religious groups because it contests their claims to be authoritative meta-narratives. Religion and, in this case, Catholicism, provides an example of the grand narrative *par excellence*. Catholicism is a narrative which situates the believer in a community with thousands of years of history and a worldwide presence.[13] The narrative also links the believer with the world to come, so the scope

9 Zygmunt Bauman, *Postmodern Ethics*. (Blackwell, Oxford, 1993), 2-37.
10 Zygmunt Bauman, 'Postmodern Religion', in Paul Heelas with David M. Martin and Paul Morris. (Eds), *Modernity and Postmodernity*. (Oxford: Blackwell, 1998), 55-78.
11 Robert Wuthnow, *After the Baby Boomers: How the Twenty-and Thirty-Somethings are Shaping the Future of American Religion*. (New Jersey: Princeton University Press, 2007), 13-17. Wuthnow acknowledges the origins of this concept to the great French anthropologist Claude Levi-Strauss's writings on the *bricoleur*.
12 Richard Usher, 'Lifelong Learning in the Postmodern', in David Aspin, Judith Chapman, Michael Hatton and Yukiko Sawano (Eds), *International Handbook of Lifelong Learning*. (Kluwers Academic Publishing: Dordrecht, 2005), 165-183.
13 John Rate, 'Challenge of Postmodernity', *Compass*, 2006, 40(2).

of the message is infinite. It speaks of life as a pilgrimage and a lifelong commitment. The call to become part of this grand narrative puts many Catholics, especially younger ones, in an unfamiliar and uncomfortable position, and one for which contemporary culture has not prepared them.

The absence of community

A feature of acceptance of the grand narrative is that it places the person into a community and, therefore, into relationship with others. The pull of contemporary culture is in the opposite direction, toward individualisation, subjectivism, and atomisation.[14] Bauman captures the sentiment of the tension between the individual and the wider community in his description of many contemporary adults as strangers for whom bonds with others, and also with culturally held norms, are transitory and tenuous.[15] Contemporary culture is a world where hope has been replaced with more cautious emotions, or to use Bauman's expression, postmodernity is a place we go "to hide from our fears" – fears about what the future will bring.[16] The harshness of the world that many of Generation X inhabit is a feature of Bauman's writing, and it can be contrasted with the more benign descriptions of authors such as Mackay who used terms such as "moral boundary riders" to describe Generation X.[17] Mackay's phrase connotes people who are in the strong position of having a number of attractive choices available to them. Hugh Bauman would see these choices as

---

14 Taylor makes a similar point when he notes that one of the most significant changes in modern culture is the movement toward subjective expressions of identity. These are fashioned by the individual as opposed to external institutional forces. See Charles Taylor, *Sources of the Self: The Making of Modern Identity*. (Cambridge: Cambridge University Press, 1992), 123-149.
15 Zygmunt Bauman, *Liquid Modernity*. (Cambridge: Polity Press, 2000), 47-93.
16 Bauman, *Imitations*, xvii.
17 Hugh Mackay, *Reinventing Australia*. (Pymble: Angus and Robertson, 1998), 1-34.

real but, nonetheless, heavily proscribed.[18] He recognised that some of the significant choices that were available to earlier generations are inaccessible or not freely available to Generation X and even less so to recent generations. Choices such as what job or career to choose or where to live are limited. Generation X, and those following them are often pitted against each other in competition, and real choice, especially for attractive and secure options, is often illusory. For many Catholics born after the Second Vatican Council, to see the Church as communion is a daunting prospect, because communion, even at a human level, is unfamiliar and, to some extent, feared.[19]

The challenges of postmodern living

Belonging to Generations X and Y brings with it a number of significant and daunting challenges, not the least of which is the establishment of a sense of identity, and a place in the world. Whereas older generations were the products of a self-confident culture that gave a clear sense of direction, Generation X and Y came to maturity in a time of relative social introspection.[20] This was true of Catholicism in countries such as Australia where the self-confidence or even triumphalism of the pre-conciliar era was replaced with uncertainty and tension. The response to living in more introspective times is not a conscious, deliberate, and resolute decision. Dealing decisively with significant issues is replaced by identification, often temporarily, with a range of uncontested options or choices.[21] The defining issues for earlier generations do not persist for Generations

---

18 Bauman, *Liquid*, 45-46.
19 Grace Davie, 'The Persistence of Institutional Religion in Modern Europe', in Linda Woodhead, Paul Heelas and David Martin, (Eds), *Peter Berger and the Study of Religion*. (London: Routledge, 2001), 101-111.
20 Wade C. Roof, *A Generation of Seekers*. (San Francisco: Harper, 1993), 27-78. David Lipsky and Alexander Abrams. *Late Bloomers: Coming of Age in America*. (New York: Times Books, 1994), 29-52.
21 Hugh Mackay, *Generations*, (Sydney: Pan Macmillan, 1997), 67-97.

X and Y because a range of responses is now considered to be acceptable. Implicit here is a loss of strong commitment to any view or affiliation with any organisation, along with a reluctance to completely disassociate from any view or group. The need to protect autonomy is paramount and acts as a type of social regulator, which prevents the individual from being too exposed to harm.[22] In the postmodern milieu, personal autonomy is, on the one hand, violated if individuals identify too closely with any of the many options available and also, on the other hand, infringed upon if one is precluded from any view or association. In this prevailing attitude, many Catholics still see themselves as part of the tradition but on their own terms, choosing what they think appropriate but never reaching a high or ongoing level of commitment.

Autonomy is also associated with freedom from commitment along with only a modest interest in ideology.[23] For post-conciliar Catholics, this translates into little concern for doctrine or prescribed behaviour. In place of commitment, more emphasis is given to the importance of human experience as a means of personal validation. Personal experience, however, does not lead to a strong sense of the collective and communal. If the personal always takes precedence over the collective, then claims of any group over the individual will always be feeble. The primacy of personal experience also leads to suspicion of ascendant institutional authority.[24] When there is no strong collective sense, maintained by recognised authority, the commitment of individuals will never be strong. This is a special problem for the Catholic Church in which the belief that God is present within the community is a pivotal doctrinal principle.

---

22 Ebaugh, *Revitalization*, 9.
23 George Barna, *Baby Busters: The Disillusioned Generation*. (Chicago: Northfield, 1994), 89-97.
24 Tom Beaudoin, *Virtual Faith*. (San Francisco: Jossey-Bass Publishers, 1998).

The cost of postmodernity

To conclude this discussion, it is important to reiterate a major insight of Bauman's that has significant pastoral implications for the new evangelisation. The lack of commitment of Generation X, and even more so Generation Y, comes at some personal cost to the individuals of these groups. Few people want to remain as strangers, forever on the periphery, lacking strong and abiding links to others.[25] The ascendency of the individual comes at some cost, a point well articulated by Mason and his colleagues. They conclude their survey of contemporary youth spirituality with this observation:

> Perhaps we should refer to them as 'individualised' rather than individualistic – it is more a fate than a choice, and more a burden than a gift, for which they and society will pay a price in years to come. They deserve and will need the understanding and support of older generations.[26]

The proliferation of choice and the phenomenon of weak group association bring insecurity, and not the real sense of community that MacLaren described as "the yearning of the post-1960s generation."[27] Those groups that are able to provide a transcendent sense of meaning and belonging, relying not on societal coercion or expectation but on other means, may provide an attractive option to some who are looking for more permanence, a way to put down roots, in a transitory world.[28] Or, to use Wilf Herberg's terminology, many may be seeking assistance in answering the fundamental existential question: "What are you?"[29] To make a choice to be strongly committed must, nonetheless,

25 Robert Wuthnow, *Sharing the Journey: Support Groups and America's New Quest for Community*. (New York: The Free Press, 1994), esp. 32-55.
26 Mason et al.., *Spirituality Among Youth in Australia* , 111-112.
27 MacLaren, *Mission Implausible*, 132.
28 Christian Smith, *American Evangelicalism: Embattled and Thriving*. (Chicago: The University of Chicago Press, 1998), proposition 8 at 116.
29 Will Herberg, *Protestant, Catholic, Jew*. (Garden City, N.Y.: Anchor, 1955).

be seen as a fulfillment of personal autonomy and not its abnegation. As Charles Taylor pointed out, a feature of contemporary culture in many Western countries is the triumph of "expressive individualism." This, above all else, highlights the importance of living out one's own humanity as a matter of personal choice.[30] The Church then must look to ways it can best present itself as a body that offers the individual a chance to be part of a much wider supportive and life-giving group which at the same time responds to and respects the individual. The new evangelisation will be advanced by those who see their role in it as one of their own choosing, and not something that they are directed to do as a corporate activity. Catholics of the future, in countries such as Australia, will identify strongly with the Church only because they have chosen to do so, and they will be agents of the new evangelisation only because this is something they want to do.

Post-Conciliar Catholics Making Choices

The religious marketplace or secularisation?

A further framework for analysing the social context for the new evangelisation is to see choice as fundamental to religion. This approach has chiefly been associated with the American sociologist Rodney Stark. His first premise is that individuals make religious choices on the basis of perceived benefit and cost. In other words, their behaviour can be understood as a rational choice and not, as held by many social theorists, as an illogical response to group pressure, lack of education, or superstitious fear.[31] In Stark's conception, religion is seen as competing in the market place for followers.[32] This

---

30 Charles Taylor, *Varieties of Religion Today: William James Revisited.* (Cambridge, Mass.: Harvard University Press, 2002), 65-96.
31 Stark and Finke, *Acts*, 85.
32 Laurence R. Iannaccone, 'The Consequences of Religious Market Regulation: Adam Smith and the Economics of Religion', *Rationality and Society*, 1991, 3, 156-177.

process has gone on for centuries and is dynamic and responsive. This view is often a counterpoint to the so-called secularisation thesis articulated by Steven Bruce and others.[33] The secularisation thesis maintains that modern Western culture is marked by the inexorable decline in religious belief and practice, evidenced most strongly in Northern Europe, and increasingly so in Britain, Canada, Australia and New Zealand.[34] Secularisation of culture has been taking place for some time, but its course has been accelerated since the 1960s. Writing from an analysis of Australian data, Mason commented, "a cultural revolution took place in Australia in the 1960s and 1970s – a rapid and major advance on the secularisation of consciousness, and … this process is continuing."[35]

In secularisation theory, while there is some dispute over the role religion plays on a personal level, there is a broader consensus on its decline as a significant social factor.[36] Overtly Christian leaders, for example, no longer have a significant impact on the political process, especially when compared with earlier eras.[37] In a secular culture, the formative influences on people are not religious in nature, and the power of religious symbols and explanations to shape meaning and behaviour is weakening.[38] This has implications for the new

33 Steven Bruce, *God is Dead: Secularisation in the West.* (Oxford: Blackwell). Bruce also offers a robust critique of Rational Choice Theory in Steven Bruce, *Choice and Reason: A Critique of Rational Choice Theory.* (Oxford: Oxford University Press).
34 *Statement of Conclusions for Meeting of Australian Bishops and the Prefects and Secretaries of Six Dicasteries of the Roman Curia*, 10, 18, 20, 22, 29, 32, and 35,56,57,60. Obtained on 12/10/2007 from: www.catholicculture.org/library/view.cfm?recnum=1046.
35 Michael Mason, The Spirituality of Young Australians, in Sylvia Collins Mayo and Pink Dandelion, (Eds), *Religion and Youth.* (Surrey: Ashgate, 2010), 55-65.
36 David Yamane, 'Secularisation on Trial: in Defense of a Neosecularisation Paradigm', *Journal for the Scientific Study of Religion*, 1997, 36:109-122.
37 David Sikkink, 'From Christian Civilization to Individual Civil Liberties: Framing Religion in the Legal Field', in Christian Smith, (Ed), *The Secular Revolution.* (Berkeley: University of California Press, 2003), 310-354.
38 Mark Chaves, 'Secularisation as Declining Religious Authority', 1994, *Social Forces*, 72(3), 749-775.

evangelisation since one of its critical aspects is the evangelisation of culture. In a country such as Australia, this is a difficult task because of the unfamiliarity of many with the Christian meta-narrative, and the difficulty that the Churches have in communicating religious meaning even to those who are part of their faith communities.

A limited discussion of secularisation theory can offer some insights into the situation of post-conciliar Catholics, especially regarding how and why they make religious choices. First, "classical" secularisation holds that religious beliefs decrease as a society evolves or modernises.[39] A number of statistically powerful studies have shown, however, that metaphysical beliefs such as belief in God have remained relatively high even in Europe. What have markedly declined are characteristically Christian beliefs, such as in a personal God, which have real life consequences as evidenced by clear demands and expectations.[40] Religious beliefs *per se* then have not disappeared, but have become more individual, less demanding, and not representative of a common creedal position.[41] Indeed, religious beliefs may emerge under the general heading of "spirituality" and are, at best, comforting rather than strongly formative.

Secularisation as a process

The view of secularisation as a process where belief becomes more individual and privatised is well summarised by Karel Dobbelaere.[42] He outlined a three dimensional model, which includes separate, but not completely independent movements. The first dimension or movement is a decline in religious practice, typically in the ritual forms

39 Peter Berger, 'Epistemological Modesty: An Interview with Peter Berger', *Christian Century*, 114, 974.
40 Grace Davie, *The Sociology of Religion*. (London: Sage Publications, 2007), 112-116.
41 Mason et al., *Generation Y*, 56.
42 Karel Dobbelaere, 'Secularisation: A Multi-Dimensional Model', *Current Sociology*, 1981, 29(2), 1-216.

of a particular group. For Catholics, this includes activities such as participation in and reception of the sacraments. Second, religious institutions become weaker in the sense that while they may maintain the allegiance of their followers, they lose their capacity to direct and influence both individuals and society at large. The final secularisation dimension involves religion becoming interior and private, an affair which results in religious beliefs becoming highly personal and eclectic and religious practice private to the point of being almost hidden.[43] This dimension or movement, in cultural terms, is gradual but one which has been occurring in many Western countries at least since the Enlightenment.

The movement of individuals from a religious perspective to a secular view is not achieved in one movement and can often take some time, even generations.[44] It is best described as a process that can be discussed from a number of theoretical perspectives. Yves Lambert offers a nine-stage model.[45] The first three stages involve a rupturing of what he calls the "vertical aspect of religion." This is where the clear referent in religious teaching to the divine and the transcendent is undermined. For Lambert, a key aspect of this stage of the secularisation process is a diminished sense of the importance of sin and of life after death. Once religious groups take on a worldly aspect, belief and expression become highly individualised and, as a result, lose their formative power. In Lambert's terminology, once religion has lost its transcendent dimension and also its communal expression, the stage is set for what he calls the "spiritual quest" –

---

43 John H. Simpson, 'Religion and the Churches', in James Curtis and Lorne Tepperman, (Eds.), *Understanding Canadian Society.* (Toronto: McGraw-Hill Ryerson, 1988), 57-94.

44 Callum G. Brown, *Religion and Society in Twentieth-Century Britain.* (Harlow, England: Pearson Longman, 2006), esp.306-324.

45 Yves Lambert, 'New Christianity, Indifference and Diffused Spiritualities', in Hugh McLeod, Werner Ustorf (Eds), *The Decline of Christendom in Western Europe, 1750-2000.* (Cambridge: Cambridge University Press, 2005). 63-77.

seen here as one stage of the secularisation process. The spiritual quest is not a resolution of religious questions but rather a gradual ebbing of the ability of religion to shape and direct life.

The quest is not resolved by some discovery or reconnection with the home tradition. Rather, the journey leads to a further distancing from communal beliefs and practices and develops into pragmatic and relativistic conceptions about the importance of religion to the individual.[46] In this view, religion is useful if it serves a purpose or if it helps in a particular situation. It does not, however, have any overriding valid truth claims or hold a superior worldview to the myriad of other views that modern culture throws up. The end result of the quest is the ninth and final stage of secularisation when religion for the individual becomes, to use Lambert's expression, "a la carte." When faced with a menu in an expensive restaurant, the individual is free to choose what he or she wants. These choices, however, reflect the prevailing cultural norms and can be anticipated by demographic indicators such as socio-economic status, level of education, and family of origin.

Benefits of religious choices

Rodney Stark challenged the idea that contemporary culture is growing more secular and argued that earlier times were just as secular as today.[47] It is a mistake to see the past as a golden age where rates of religious practice and affiliation were much higher. The remarkably high rate of religious participation by Catholics, in Australia and elsewhere, in the immediate post-war era would be explained by Stark as an unusual confluence of factors which made religious affiliation

---

46 Christian Smith with Patricia Snell, *Souls in Transition: The Religious and Spiritual Lives of Emerging Adults.* (New York: Oxford University Press, 2009), 252.
47 Theodore Caplow, *All Faithful People: Change and Continuity in Middletown's Religion.* (Minneapolis: University of Minnesota Press, 1983).

attractive. Some of these included high conflict with the surrounding culture, strong metaphysical compensators, internal social cohesion, and high birth rates.[48] Historically, this situation was not typical.[49]

Levels of religious commitment have fluctuated over time. Religious groups can emerge quickly if they meet perceived needs and also fall away suddenly if they no longer fulfil a need.[50] From this argument flow two important principles. First, for individuals to make the choice to associate with religious groups there must be some perceived benefit.[51] Indeed, the greater the benefit the stronger the commitment. There are many benefits that accrue from being part of a group, such as social networking, shared activities, and assistance in times of need. A primary incentive for affiliation, however, is a perception that the religious group facilitate: an "exchange with the gods."[52] Through association with a religious group, an individual should be able to have an active relationship with the gods, one that brings with it unique benefits.

However, Churches today function in a culture where belief in God is challenged.[53] Bernard Lonergan refers to five specific challenges: antiquated theology, demythologisation of Scripture, the thrust of modern philosophy, the collapse of Catholicism, and a softening of the dogmatic component of Catholic theology.[54] In the face of these challenges, one of the principal tasks of Churches

---

48 James D. Davidson, *Catholicism in Motion: The Church in American Society.* (Ligouri, Missouri: Ligouri Publications, 2005), 162.
49 Rodney Stark, 'Secularisation R.I.P' in William H. Swatos and Daniel V. Olson (Eds), *The Secularisation Debate.* (Lanham, Maryland: Rowman & Littlefield Publishers), 47.
50 Finke and Stark, *Churching,* 156-197.
51 Rodney Stark and William Sims Bainbridge, *A Theory of Religion.* (New York: Peter Lang, 1987), 27.
52 Stark and Finke, *Acts,* 91.
53 Bernard Lonergan, 'The Absence of God in Modern Culture' in Ryan and Tyrell, (Eds), *Second Collection,* 109-111.
54 Bernard Lonergan, 'Natural Knowledge of God' in Ryan and Tyrell, (Eds), *Second Collection,* 117-133.

should be to constantly make the case for the connection between the faith community and the divine, for this is what the Churches have to offer. In contemporary culture, the Church's role in maintaining an ongoing connection with the divine is most imperilled. When this occurs Churches can become just a sociological phenomenon, lacking the vital connection with God, which in Catholic terms is communion through Christ.

In terms of seeing religion as a rational choice, a loss of emphasis on the divine in religious groups is a grave situation, not only for theological reasons, but because the group is tampering with the essential benefit that comes from being a member. If the connection with the divine is lost, one likely scenario is that religious groups lose the power to attract and retain strong communal allegiance. This has direct implications for the long-term viability of religious institutions such as Catholic schools. In addition individual beliefs become more personal and eclectic, typical of a secularised culture. In Stark's argument, religion will not entirely disappear, but will remain dormant until religious groups again offer something of high cost and value.

Religious choice as minimising costs

Another principle of what Stark calls "Rational Choice Theory" (RCT), which is of great relevance to the new evangelisation in Catholic schools, is that the individual will seek to minimise the cost of association with a group without decreasing the perceived benefits.[55] If a religious group becomes just a human fellowship, it competes with a large number of other groups, each of which could perhaps offer greater benefits. For example, Generation X and Y Catholics are part of a large cohort that in much of the Church's contemporary pastoral practice capitalises on the perceived importance of inclusion.

---

55 Stark and Finke, *Acts*, 100.

In terms of RTC, many Catholics effectively manage to reduce the cost of religious affiliation without losing any of the benefits. They avoid an existential void by identifying, albeit loosely, with a historically significant group. They do not need to confront major existential questions alone. To use a postmodern term, they have a place in a meta-narrative if they should desire it.

There is also a range of very practical benefits. Post-conciliar Catholics can maintain, if they wish, a strong familial religious connection. They can celebrate Christmas with their families by going to Mass. If they wish, they can marry in a church, bury their parents in a religious service, send their children to Catholic schools, and associate with a wide range of people who are very much like them. All of this can be gained for very little cost. There is no requirement to attend services, hold difficult or challenging beliefs, give up a substantial portion of their income, or take part in any ritual or process that may stigmatise them. In these circumstances, it is not surprising that many post-conciliar Catholics choose not to disaffiliate formally from Church membership, at least for the time being, when it offers so much and allows the individual so much freedom. It seems rational, therefore, that the inexorable pull on most post-conciliar Catholics is toward a loose form of affiliation.[56] As a result, any new evangelisation program in Catholic schools must provide some compelling reason for Catholics to move beyond an exchange relationship where they perceive great benefit in preserving the *status quo*.

What is to be done?

To conclude this discussion, a key question focuses on what religious groups can do to challenge the *status quo*. In terms of Stark's

---

56 Hechter comments that a rational person will not join an organisation if he or she can reap the benefits of membership without participating. Michael Hechter, *Principles of Group Solidarity.* (Philadelphia: Temple University Press, 1987), 27.

argumentation, they should strongly emphasise their transcendent elements and most especially their connection with the gods. Furthermore, they need to emphasise that this connection can only be maintained by membership in the group, and that this discipleship brings with it high expectations, but also metaphysical compensation. RTC argues that religious groups need to make demands, since the natural inclination of people is to minimise the costs associated with association and to become what some have called "free riders."[57] Strong religious affiliation is sustained further when individuals can readily use supernatural categories to describe their lives.[58] So when group members pray, for example, they should see this as a form of communication with God, where God listens and responds. Because of these interactions, God is seen to be alive in their lives and can influence their behaviour. The lesson here for the new evangelisation is to stress its metaphysical claims – a closer and more intimate connection between the believer and the divine *logos*. This has especial relevance for religious education in Catholic schools, a point that will be discussed in greater detail in the final chapter. In a general sense, a recent tendency in Catholicism to demythologise key teachings should be recognised, and every opportunity to re-sacralise beliefs and actions should be taken.[59] Attending Mass, for example, should be seen as an expression of the theological reality of Christ as the source of communion with each other and with God.

---

57 Laurence R. Iannaccone, 'Sacrifice and Stigma: Reducing Free-Riding in Cults, Communes and Other Collectives', *Journal of Political Economy*, 1992, 100(2), 271-292.
58 Gary Bouma, *Religion: Meaning, Transcendence and Community in Australia.* (Melbourne: Longman Cheshire, 1992), 63-91.
59 Randall Collins, 'H. Paul Douglas Lecture. The Four M's of Religion: Magic, Membership, Morality and Mysticism', *Review of Religious Research*, 2008, 50(1), 5-15.

Post-Conciliar Catholics and Vicarious Religion

> I believe in a higher power than myself. I'm not sure if it's God yet,
> but I do believe in something – that there's a higher power. There
> is something which I can leave things to, let go of those things –
> this higher power takes care of. – *Jarl, a 41-year old Swede.*[60]

A diminishing God

Another perspective on the weakening association of post-conciliar
Catholics with the Church is offered in the writings of Grace Davie.
Davie wrote from a European perspective, coining the phrase
"believing without belonging."[61] In this view, belief is best understood
by fairly generic metaphysical categories, rather than orthodox
Christian beliefs such as acceptance of a Trinitarian and personal
God.[62] In these terms, most Europeans, as exemplified by Jarl in the
quotation provided above, are believers because the alternative, a stark
atheism, is not a position with which many are comfortable identifying,
a point made by a number of influential modern theologians.[63] One
reason that Benedict XVI has been such a promoter of the new
evangelisation is that it responds so closely to his own analysis of
the ideological roots of religious disaffiliation, especially in Europe,
which he sees as a deeply seated turning away from God initially on
a conceptual level but more importantly in how they live their lives.
This point is taken up by others who stress the praxis of atheism over
the idea of it. Dorothee Solle, for example, argued that atheism needs
to be re-conceptualised to avoid overemphasising its ideological or

---

60 Phil Zuckerman, *Society Without God: What the Least Religious Nations on Earth Can Tell Us About Contentment.* (New York: New York University Press, 2008), 129

61 Grace Davie, *Religion in Britain since 1945: Believing Without Belonging.* (Oxford: Blackwell, 1994).

62 David Voas and Andrew Crockett, 'Religion in Britain: Neither Believing nor Belonging', *Sociology,* 2005, 39: 11-28.

63 Henri de Lubac, *The Drama of Atheistic Humanism.* (New York: New American Library, 1963), 5.

philosophical basis. She pointed out that the classical distinctions between atheism and theism are no longer relevant or descriptive.[64] One reason for this is that many Europeans are, in effect, living out a form of pragmatic atheism, which does not see itself as a counterpoint to any ideological or theological position. In distinguishing between three kinds of atheism, Kasper supported this idea. He described the most prevalent form of atheism, at least in a European context, as a practical one, which is not a denial of God but which regards an indifference to God as the plausible stance to take.[65] An important manifestation of this attitude is a willingness to agree with what Solle saw as superficial questions such as, "Do you believe in God?" but bewilderment with more substantive questions that make real demands on belief and action.[66] This has a parallel in Davie's terminology where belonging, as typified by participation in Church rituals or strong identification with the Church, is markedly on the decline. Thus, religious affiliation acts as a metaphorical safety net. Its main purpose is to help people in difficult times, but it is not an active or formative influence. Brown described this very restricted use of religion in times of crisis as an example of its "functional irrelevance" in the lives of many people.[67] Like all safety nets, it is not designed or supposed to be used too often, but it gives a sense of reassurance and if removed would make life more uncertain and anxious.

Benign religious affiliation

This idea of religion as a safety net can be extended to a generalised argument about the nature of religious belief in contemporary

---

64 Dorothee Solle, *Thinking About God: An Introduction to Theology.* (Philadelphia: Trinity Press International, 1990), 171-182.
65 Walter Kasper, *The God of Jesus Christ.* (New York: Crossroad, 1996), esp. 7-12.
66 Kasper, *Jesus Christ*, 183-195, at 186.
67 L.B. Brown, *The Psychology of Religious Belief.* (Orlando, FL.: Academic Press, 1987). 217.

culture. The attitude of many Catholics to the Church is not hostile. The typical pattern of religious socialisation has been weak and has left few scars. The Church exists and this is a good thing. Many feel in some way part of it, albeit, in a distant sense. Having the Church there makes people feel comfortable; it is reassuring to know that there are committed religious believers as long as there is no expectation that one must join them. This attitude has been called vicarious religion, which Davie defined as "the willingness of the population to delegate the religious sphere to the professional ministry of the state Churches."[68] In terms of the new evangelisation, this delegation of responsibility results inevitably, if not immediately, in a loss of personal connection to the faith community. Given the choice, few people would want a metaphysical safety net removed. One of the strongest manifestations of this religious affiliation is in the Nordic countries and Germany. In these countries, people pay substantial taxes to keep Churches running in some style. Bureaucracies are staffed, buildings, especially Churches, are maintained, and special events funded. The population takes great civic pride in preserving their heritage, and does not want to see the substantial signs of the past disappear. There is, however, in terms of Christian commitment, a Potemkin quality about all of this. Religion does not play a significant part in the lives of most people. The exception is, perhaps, in times of crisis, such as a disaster or the death of a popular public figure, or at significant life transition points. This sentiment is well captured in following quote, provided by Bibby:

> Some observers maintain that few people today are actually abandoning their religious traditions. Rather, they draw selective beliefs and practices, even if they do not attend services frequently. They are not about to be recruited by other religious groups. Their

---

68 Grace Davie, *Religion in Modern Europe: A Memory Mutates.* (Oxford: Oxford University Press, 2000), 59.

identification with the religious tradition is fairly solidly fixed, and it is to these groups that they will turn when confronted with marriage, death and, frequently, birth.[69]

Amongst Canadian Catholics, 61% found this statement accurate. A further 31% found it somewhat accurate.[70]

The chain of memory

Vicarious religion also serves as a link to the historical memory of religion.[71] It is a tenuous link to a meta-narrative that no longer figures in the lives of many who cannot, nonetheless, bring themselves to part from it entirely. In ways that are difficult to articulate, the religious memory connects the immediate to the ultimate, and this is what gives it its enduring quality. To live without these chains, or rather to live when these chains have been suddenly severed, is to be rootless and drifting in a sea of indistinguishable choices and possibilities – a very postmodern image. Over time, other chains of memory will emerge, and individuals will re-orientate themselves to a new reality based on the bonds that have developed to replace the old ones. This process takes time and can be unsettling, so it is no surprise that many in Western countries seek to keep alive the memories that they have. It is unlikely, however, that these bonds will ever become strong and compelling in the sense that they have a direct or decisive influence on how people live.

The idea of vicarious religion offers many insights into the world of post-conciliar Catholics. It explains church attendance on special occasions: it is important for individuals to mark these events as reminders of a different reality that can be re-entered when necessary.

69 Reginald W. Bibby, 'Secularisation and Change' in W.E. Hewitt, (Ed), *The Sociology of Religion: A Canadian Focus*. (Toronto: Butterworths, 1993), 65-80, at 79.
70 Hewitt, *Sociology of Religion*, 79.
71 Daniele Hervieu Leger, *Religion as a Chain of Memory*. (New Jersey: Rutgers University Press, 2000).

Perhaps more significantly, it offers an explanation for the continued popularity of Catholic schools.[72] Catholic schools in Australia exist as, perhaps, the most tangible part of the general religious memory. For an interlude of years they have provided a daily point of contact between the Church – once or twice removed – and the individual. Parents send their children to Catholic schools for many reasons, but religious formation is not the primary or even secondary one. Flynn has shown that in a five point forced response, parents consistently place religious considerations last as their reason for choosing Catholic schools.[73] Nonetheless, they like having Catholic schools available, and would oppose any initiative that would make them less accessible. We see here, again, the vicarious principle in action: that which in their regular lives is absent is present at the school. Parents and students may feel comfortable, for example, with symbols such as religious pictures and crucifixes around the school even if these are not present in the home.

Catholic schools also offer a sense of history and continuity, and keeping alive the religious memory in a very concrete way. For many families, earlier generations may have gone to the same school as well as siblings. Many Catholics feel that it is beneficial for their children to have some mild religious instruction, and develop a

---

72 Anthony Spencer of the Pastoral Research Centre Trust notes that in England and Wales many parents have their children baptised specifically to get them into Catholic schools, which are seen as a more academic alternative. This explains a curious "bump" in figures for late baptisms, a 5% increase against a steady decline in total number of baptisms. It is also worth recording that figures in the study for Catholic participation in the three "rites of passage" – baptism, marriage, and funerals – has fallen 23% since 1958, with marriage the most affected. Spencer comments that the decline is "pretty horrific." Anthony Spencer, 'Children Baptised to get into Catholic schools', *Daily Telegraph*, Obtained on 14/1/2008 at: http://www.telegraph.co.uk/news/main.jhtml?xml=/news/2008/01/12/ncdu312.xml.

73 Marcellin Flynn, *The Culture of Catholic Schools: A Study of Catholic Schools, 1972-1993.* (Homebush, NSW: St. Paul's Publications), 171. Students' religious expectations are similar. Of the 12 lowest priorities for Catholic schools, 11 listed by students were of a religious nature, 164.

homogenous moral sense that they attribute to the school imparting certain values. Along with this are also taught inoffensive and largely generic religious views.[74] One day, however, this association with the school will end and it will not be replaced by a connection with the worshipping community of faith, since this would involve too high a level of commitment.

In the shorter term, however, the existence of relatively large numbers of Catholics who have exercised a choice to retain a loose level of affiliation, or to use the safety net of vicarious religion, presents at least two important consequences for the new evangelisation. On the one hand, these people have retained a connection with the faith community, albeit loose and often on their own terms. They are not hostile to the faith tradition and may be open to being invited to a deeper commitment. In terms of pastoral outreach, this situation is easier than reaching out to Catholics or others who have no connection whatsoever with the faith community. On the other hand, large numbers of loosely connected yet satisfied members make the task of renewal difficult. At the very least, it makes change harder to implement because there is no immediately felt need for it. The new evangelisation as envisaged by John Paul II sets for itself a demanding standard, that of closer union with Christ and a desire to tell others about this. Any Catholic agency, and certainly Catholic schools, that seeks to play a role in the new evangelisation will face a difficult task, as many members of the community will not see the need for such a renewal. One of the most powerful options that Catholics today can exercise is the choice to remain a member of the faith community in a loose sense, one that guarantees them a right to their own personal, private, and ineffable spirituality that does not, amongst other things, lead to adherence to common creedal positions.

---

74 Mason et al., *Generation Y*, 55.

Six Features of the Contemporary Cultural Landscape and Some of Their Implications for the New Evangelisation

To draw together by way of summary some of the themes developed in the discourse in this chapter, six points are now made.

First, the Church in countries such as Australia has been relatively successful in giving many people a loose sense of affiliation and, in many ways, the wider culture supports this type of connection. With regard to the new evangelisation, however, a number of difficulties present themselves. In ecclesiological terms, Bonhoeffer's warnings about the Church as a dispenser of "cheap grace" could well apply here.[75] The Church of the loosely affiliated certainly does not closely resemble a community of disciples. It lacks the metaphysical dimension of Church where members are united with each other and with the Church in Christ and through the Holy Spirit. For many, being part of the Church has become a sociological exercise with no obvious supernatural dimension. The dangers of this are apparent in the loss of the uniqueness of the Christian message. The words of Pope Benedict XVI that "the crisis of the Church is a crisis of the absence of God," are quite telling.

Second, the Church needs to reconceptualise many of its pastoral strategies and sense of its mission in the light of its current disposition.[76] What is needed now, in broad terms, is a strengthening and reinvigorating of the Body of Christ and a renewed perception that Christian belief and commitment are reasonable positions. The need for this renewal is one of the founding assumptions of what

---

75 Bonhoeffer, *Discipleship*, 1-64.
76 Gabriel Moran, *Vision and Tactics: Toward an Adult Church*. (New York: Herder and Herder, 1968), 143-147; Callum G. Brown, *The Death of Christian Britain: Understanding Secularisation 1800-2000*. (London: Routledge, 2001),166-169.

Dulles has called "post-critical theology."[77] Post-critical theology arises out of an awareness that the fundamental relationship between the wider culture and the Church has changed, largely in terms of a disproportionate power relationship, where the Church lacks the capacity to engage with culture on an equal footing. The Church has lost its privileged position, has become one voice among many, and to be heard must be able to articulate its message with power and conviction. It needs to be clearly re-stated that religious beliefs can be firmly held by reasonable people. Dulles put this well when he wrote: "Our contemporaries, well aware that religious tenets are capable of being questioned, need to be shown how firm religious commitments may nevertheless be responsible."[78]

Third, a feature of all the theoretical frameworks discussed in this chapter is that they describe many Catholics as being on the periphery of the Church and that they may have no real inclination to change this state of affairs.[79] As religious consumers, many have made a strong bargain, which precludes a high level of religious commitment. Many have experienced, in their view, what Catholicism has to offer, taken what they want from it and seem to be more than content with their current position or the choices they have made. To many, Frank O'Loughlin's assessment of Christian affiliation in Australia could apply: "Many people continue to call themselves Christian, but they give that word a meaning so weakened that the traces of its roots in Christ and his Gospel are hard to find."[80] A very pertinent question arises as to what is the best pastoral and strategic approach to take

---

77 Avery Dulles, *The Craft of Theology: From Symbol to System*. (New York: Crossroad, 1995), 3-17.
78 Dulles, *Craft of Theology*, 6.
79 Callum G. Brown, *Religion and Society in Twentieth-Century Britain*. (Harlow, England: Pearson Longman, 2006), 316.
80 Frank O'Loughlin, 'The New Evangelisation of the Twenty First Century', *The Australasian Catholic Record*, 2007, 401-413, at 408.

when dealing with people who have assimilated a Christian sensibility, but do not display the deep inner conversion that is at the heart of the new evangelisation? It should be recognised and acknowledged that ministry to this group is difficult. Ministry needs to be carefully conceived, while success may be best measured in small incremental steps and targeted toward specific groups.

Fourth, in their excellent study of generations of American Catholics, D'Antonio and his colleagues interspersed well-presented quantitative data with a series of dialogues between a hypothetical mother and daughter. One represented a more socialised, highly committed Catholic and the other was more typical of the Generation X/Y pattern. A critical question arises as to what the granddaughter, the next generation of Catholic, will contribute to this dialogue? Is the existence of large numbers of loosely affiliated Catholics indicative of a consistent pattern that will continue into the future, or is it a more terminal scenario, where following generations drift out of the Catholic orbit altogether? For Callum Brown, this question has been answered conclusively.[81] He proposed a three generational process of religious disaffiliation from the mainline Christian Churches in Britain. The third generation becomes thoroughly secular in the sense that their worldviews and opinions are indistinguishable from the general public. In terms of the theoretical positions presented in this Chapter, there is some support for this notion. The individualisation and uncertainly of postmodernity, for example, seem likely to continue.[82]

A similar argument could be made about the other benefits of maintaining a loose religious connection. Writing about the future

---

81 Brown, *Death of Christian Britain*, 189-194.
82 Grace Davie, 'Europe the Exception That Proves the Rule?' in Peter L. Berger, (Ed) The *Desecularisation of the World: Resurgent Religion and World Politics*. (Grand Rapids, Mich: William B. Eerdmans, 1999), 65-83 at 83.

of Catholicism in Quebec, a community that has experienced a dramatic decline in religious practice, Christiano noted that while the historical place of Catholicism is recognised, most Quebecers had an ever-weakening connection with these historical roots.[83] He observed, "whether future generations of Quebecers, more than ever imbued with the secular attitudes of their most accomplished artistic, intellectual, and economic elites (if not the critical foundations of those attitudes), will find such loose attachments to religious tradition either useful or ultimately satisfying is still an open question."[84] In terms of vicarious religion, what happens when the historical memory of faith becomes very weak, or the number of committed Christians becomes so small that not even they can keep alive the sense of faith for others?

Fifth, it seems that many Generation X and Generation Y Catholics are, to use Rahner's analogy, somewhere in the middle, as the Church changes from a national Church where membership was automatic, if unreflective, to one where individuals make a personal decision to be associated.[85] At the very least, this realisation must make the Church more attuned to responding in a proactive way by encouraging people to become part of the faith community and to nurture those already affiliated. The era of uncritical, almost passive, enculturation has ended. Evangelisation is not an option as much as a necessity in a culture where options abound. There may be a suggestion of a way forward in Mary Jo Neitz's study of charismatic Catholics. She pointed out that these people have chosen a particular

83 Kevin J. Christiano, 'The Trajectory of Catholicism in Twentieth-Century Quebec', in Leslie Woodcock Tentler, (Ed), *The Church Confronts Modernity: Catholicism since 1950 in the United States, Ireland and Quebec.* (Washington D.C.: The Catholic University of America Press, 2007), 21-61.
84 Tentler, *Confronts Modernity.* 61.
85 Karl Rahner, *Shape*, 50.

"religious reality."[86] They have done so, in the face of many options, because they see this as an attractive and life-giving decision. They are not overwhelmed by choice if something stands out as exceptional. Here, choosing to be a Christian is a mark of discipleship rather than of tribalism, so this is in accord with the ecclesiology that underpins the new evangelisation. In keeping with the notion of the religious consumer, Wuthnow commented that many young adults today are in a bargaining position, not just with religious affiliation but with many other aspects of their lives, and an important factor in this bargaining is perceived benefit.[87]

The Church faces the challenge of having to articulate a message and a rationale to a no longer captive audience. If we accept this notion of the Church needing to take a more evangelistic tone, in the sense of proclaiming its mission to a more disconnected, distracted, and discerning audience, one important consequence concerns those who hear and accept this message, who respond to the call of the new evangelisation. They are likely to display the characteristic of the religiously highly committed. They are not Catholic because their parents were or because they drifted into this unreflectively. They have made a decision to join or to remain a part of the faith community. They are likely to see themselves as disciples of Christ in the terms spelled out in the new evangelisation of Pope John Paul II. They could also be described, using Lonergan's terminology, of having fallen in love with God. For them, the call to evangelise and to ever deepen their relationship with Christ will be a priority. One significant consequence of the emergence of this group is the way in which the wider Church deals with them. They are coming into a Church that is still very much in transition from a monopoly to a community of conviction.

---

86 Neitz, *Charisma*, 257-258.
87 Wuthnow, *Baby Boomers*, 217.

It may be that their zeal and ardour is viewed with suspicion by some. They take religion seriously. In a culture where religion is accepted most readily in its benign and private forms, those who take on a much stronger commitment may not always be received with enthusiasm, even by some in their own faith community. They do, after all, have some resemblance to St. Paul, who experienced perhaps history's most famous exogenous conversion experience. He is presented in *Redemptoris Missio* as the human exemplar for the new evangelisation. Paul of Tarsus was a figure who challenged others to a higher standard and to move out of what had become comfortable and complacent positions. Even a brief perusal of the Acts of the Apostles indicates that Paul was not always greeted with open arms either by the Jewish or Roman officials or the nascent Christian communities.

Sixth, and finally, at least for the short to medium term, the number of Catholics who express a loose affiliation with the Church will remain quite large, for the reasons outlined in this Chapter. It would be perilous to take this as some kind of vindication of current pastoral strategies. The fact that, for example, demands for places in Catholic schools remain high is not an indicator of resurgence in strong religious commitment on the part of parents.[88] Indeed, enrolment patterns in Catholic schools could change. In the United States overall, Catholic school enrollment now stands at about 2.3 million, down from the peak of 5.2 million in the early 1960s.[89] In Canada, both Newfoundland and Quebec, provinces with at least nominal Catholic majorities, have abolished funding to Catholic

---

88 It is especially perilous to see participation in Catholic schools as some type of alterative to Mass attendance. See Cashen, *Sacred Heart*, 189; Maurice Ryan, 'Future Catholic Schools: Exclusive, Inclusive and Plural Options. *Journal of Religious Education*, 2008, 56(4), 21-28.
89 *Catholic School Enrollment Dwindling*. Obtained on 9/4/2008 from http://www.usatoday.com/news/education/2008-04-09-catholic-schools_N.html.

schools, a move undertaken without widespread protest.[90] Catholic schools seem especially vulnerable if parents are sending their children to them for a variety of reasons which are not primarily religious. This places them in direct competition with other schools. If parents are greatly concerned with the religious aspect of Catholic schools, then this is a relatively stable clientele. Other schools cannot provide this educational dimension. They can, however, provide other educational experiences and if these are placed ahead of the religious dimension of the school in the eyes of most parents, then enrolment in Catholic schools could fluctuate according to shifts in demand.

One particular challenge for Catholic schools is how best to assist in the catechesis of young people. There is a distinction, recognised in the discussion of the new evangelisation in *Redemptoris Missio*, that catechesis is a distinct process from evangelisation. Nonetheless, they remain complementary and in the new evangelisation the boundaries between the two activities become blurred.[91] Catechesis and evangelisation, therefore, often occur in tandem in the Church's missionary outreach, and certainly as it is expressed in Catholic schools. A key insight of Catholic educational philosophy is that knowing more about faith can lead to the strengthening of faith. Schools, therefore, have a role to play in catechesis, but it is a complementary one. Catechesis must be situated within a faith community. The family, in particular, is the seat of catechesis.

Concluding Comments

Beyer has commented that much of how Catholics see themselves and live out their faith could be described as cultural Catholicism, which is typified by "a diffuse spiritual quest, emotional and largely

---

90 James T. Mulligan, *Catholic Education: Ensuring a Future.* (Ottawa: Novalis, 2005), 108-113.
91 Congregation for Catholic Education, *The Religious Dimension of Education in a Catholic School.* (Sydney: St. Paul Publications, 1988).

unorganised or even haphazard practice."[92] Leaving aside the issue of its longevity, there is little chance that cultural Catholicism in countries such as Australia will provide the energy needed for revitalisation and growth. The new evangelisation, however, is a proposal that responds directly to this critical issue of how to re-engage Catholics and encourage high levels of commitment amongst more than a relative few of its members.

This Chapter has argued that significant social factors posed by postmodernity make strong and lasting allegiance to any group problematic. Most Catholics can choose a religious niche for themselves which maximises benefits but precludes cost. From this position they are unlikely to move to more demanding levels of commitment. The insights of vicarious religion suggest that most are satisfied with an understated Christian presence in society that gives them options and provides a safety net in times of crisis, and also allows for the religious chains of memory to be maintained, however tenuously. This discussion has led to six features of contemporary culture in countries like Australia, which make the task of the new evangelisation challenging. If we take these factors together, a reasonable conclusion is that the Church in the future will be numerically smaller than it is today. This decline could be precipitous once the pre-conciliar generation passes away. In many ways, the cultural forces at work cultivate loose religious affiliation. In the light of decreasing numbers and a non-supportive culture, the new evangelisation can be seen as an appropriate and timely reading of the signs of the times and a critical engagement with the wider culture.

If the social conditions are right for low levels of religious

---

92 Peter Beyer, 'Roman Catholicism in Contemporary Quebec: The Ghosts of Religion Past?' in W.E. Hewitt, (Ed), *The Sociology of Religion: A Canadian Focus.* (Toronto: Butterworths, 1993), 133-156, at 153.

commitment, a critical issue becomes: how is strong commitment, over what can be termed conventional levels, to be encouraged and nurtured? Following from this, at least in a theoretical sense, what are the factors that are most relevant for a discussion of the new evangelisation in Catholic schools? Before undertaking to address these questions, however, some comments will be made reevaluating the new evangelisation in terms of contemporary critique. The new evangelisation, like any concept, much less a program of action, is subject to some critical reflection. Some of these challenges will be addressed in the next Chapter. This discussion will also draw out some of the implications of the new evangelisation as well as recapitulating some of its key features. As such, it is a prelude to the final Chapter, which discusses specific principles of the new evangelisation as they apply to Catholic schools.

4

Some Perceived Difficulties with the New Evangelisation

Introduction

Before raising some of the specific issues and challenges of the new evangelisation for Catholic schools, a review of some of the issues, both latent and manifest, that have been raised so far is in order. This review takes the form of addressing some of the critiques of the new evangelisation from a range of perspectives. In addressing these concerns, it is intended that some of the arguments presented earlier can be examined again, but this time in a new configuration.

Is a New Evangelisation Really Necessary?

> If I were a religious leader, I would be troubled by the facts and figures currently describing the lives of young Americans, their involvement in congregations, and their spiritual practices.[1]

Throughout this book, an assumption has been made that the Church, in Australia and elsewhere, is in need of revitalisation.[2] Indeed, the whole basis of the new evangelisation is that significant numbers of Catholics have lost a Christian sense, and need to be reconnected with the Church. From this position a number of implications follow. The Church, in places such as Australia, does not currently experience

---

1 Wuthnow, *Baby Boomers*, 214.

2 Benedict XVI lends his weight to this assessment when he comments: "This is certainly a form of suffering which, I would say, fits into our time in history, and in which we generally see that the so-called 'great' Churches seem to be dying. This is true particularly in Australia, also in Europe, but not so much in the United States." Benedict XVI, Address to Diocesan Clergy of Aosta: On Critical Issues in the Life of the Church (ZE05081620, 2005-08-16). Obtained 9/12/2007 from: http://zenit.org/article-13717?l=english.

vigorous health – the new Pentecost anticipated at the Council has not yet arrived. The Church also needs to reach out to those on its periphery. These views are, however, misguided if the state of Catholic life is much stronger than assumed. This argument is, perhaps, best put by the prolific American sociologist, Andrew Greeley. He argued:

> There is no evidence of a decline in American religious belief and practice or of the importance of religion for the rest of American life over the last half century with the exception of some severe jolts to Catholicism (caused by the birth control encyclical rather than the Vatican Council).[3]

Greeley speaks from an American perspective.[4] Data indicates that the rate of religious belief and practice among Americans is far higher than for other Western countries and this may affect any analysis and strategic planning. To use Mass attendance rates among Catholic teenagers as one example, McCorquodale and her colleagues reported that 39% of U.S. teenagers (13 to 17 years old) attend Mass at least once a week.[5] Dixon reported that for a comparable group of Australia teenagers aged 15-19, the weekly Mass attendance figure is around 12%.[6] The intention here is not to provide a lengthy comparison between the United States and other countries but to simply note

---

3 Andrew M. Greeley, 'Religion After 2000'. Obtained on 8/5/2002 from www. agreeley.com/articles/re12000.html. For an Australian variant of this argument see Cashen, *Sacred Heart*, esp. 183-192, 215-219. He dismisses talk of a crisis as "doom and gloom". As Greeley's position is far better known, it is examined in detail here.
4 It can be noted here but Greeley has adopted a similar logic in his support of American Catholic schools arguing that they have a discernable impact on a range of measures. See Andrew Greeley, William McCreay and Ken McCourt, *Catholic Schools in a Declining Church*. (Kansas City: Sheed and Ward. 1986). Others disagree, especially those working outside the United States. See Leslie J. Francis, 'Roman Catholic Secondary Schools: Falling Rolls and Pupil Attitudes', *Educational Studies*, 1986, 12, 119-127.
5 Charlotte McCorquodale, Victoria Shepp and Leigh Sterten, *National Study of Youth and Religion: Analysis of the Population of Catholic Teenagers and Their Parents*, (Washington D.C.: National Federation for Catholic Youth Ministry, 2004), 15.
6 Dixon, *Community*, 96.

the difference.[7] A large number of studies have shown a decline in religious belief and practice over time in a range of countries.[8] Nonetheless, even from an American perspective, Greeley's argument can be challenged.[9]

Australia appears to have much more in common with patterns of religious belief and practice in European countries such as England and Wales, rather than with the United States.[10] Even if we concede that the immediate post-war period was something of an anomaly in terms of religious practice, there are still grounds for serious concern that justify an emphasis on evangelisation. Admittedly, this is not to capitulate to an unfounded pessimism. Indeed, terms such as optimism and pessimism have a moral connotation and may not be helpful descriptors. A better term could be "realistic": are these concerns based on a *realistic* assessment of all the information we have at our disposal? Some comparative data illustrates this point and also the challenge facing the Church. Tom Horwood reported the following Mass attendance rates for Catholics in England and Wales, the data representing a count figure for one weekend in autumn:[11]

---

7 Mason et al., *Generation Y*, 327, 319.
8 The following give an indication of the breadth of research confirming this point. Michael Hill and Richard Bowman, 'Religious Adherence and Religious Practice in Contemporary New Zealand', *Archives de Sciences Sociales des Religions*, 1985, 59, 91-112; Reginald W. Bibby, 'Religionless Christianity: A Profile of Religion and Convergence in the Canadian 80s', *Social Indicators Research*, 198, 2, 169-181; Eva M. Hamberg, 'On Stability and Change in Religious Beliefs, Practice and Attitudes: A Swedish Panel Study', *Journal for the Scientific Study of Religion*, 1991, 30, 63-80.
9 See, for example, Mark Chaves, 'Secularisation and Religious Revival: Evidence from U.S. Church Attendance Rates', *Journal for the Scientific Study of Religion*, 1989, 28, 464-477.
10 Martin groups Australia with Canada and New Zealand in having a similar religiosity. David Martin, *On Secularisation: Towards a Revised General Theory*. (Aldershot: Hants Ashgate, 2005), 94-97.
11 Tom Horwood, *The Future of the Catholic Church in Britain*. (England: Laicos Press, 2006), 13.

Table 3: Mass attendance rates in England and Wales 1961-2001

Year	Mass attendance	% of Catholic population
1961	1,941,900	53.1
1971	1,925,000	46.7
1981	1,644,224	38.6
1991	1,292,312	30.4
2001	994,181	24.0

In a similar vein, Horwood reported a decline of 55% in the yearly number of Catholic baptisms over the forty-year period. In the same period, the number of adult receptions into the Church fell from approximately 14,000 to 5,500.[12] During the same interval, the number of marriages conducted in a Catholic Church fell by more than half.[13] In comparison, Dixon provided the following Australian data. In 2001, a national count of attendees revealed that 15.3% of Australia's Catholic population, or 765,000 people, attended Mass on a typical weekend.[14] This represented a decline from the 1996 figure of 11.5%, or just under 100,000 – approximately 20,000 per year. The decline figure for those aged between 25 and 34, the cusp of Generation X and Y, was more than twice the average.[15] The number of baptisms has also fallen steadily from 71,000 in 1993 to 58,300 in 2002.[16] In 2002, the number of marriages between two Catholics was

---

12 In a similar vein, contrasting eras, McDermott notes that in the period 1946-1964, the Catholic Church in the United States registered 2,368,795 converts. John M. McDermott, 'Introduction' in McDermott and Gavin, *Pope John Paul II* , 5.

13 Horwood, *Future*, 14-17.

14 Dixon, *Community*, 95. In 2006 the average Mass attendance rate for Australian Catholics had declined to 13.8%. This figure is a prelude to much lower figures in the future as the highest attendance was for the 75-79 age cohort, 35.6%, and the lowest for the 20-24 cohort 5.4%. This information derived from the 2006 count of Mass attendees was provided in a personal communication from Robert Dixon, Director Bishops Office for Pastoral Planning, November 20, 2007.

15 Dixon, *Community*, 97.

16 Dixon, *Community*, 111.

35% lower than in 1991, while the number of marriages involving one Catholic partner dropped by 37% in the same period.[17]

Markers of identity

These figures show a clear decline in the reception of key sacraments, a significant marker of Catholic identity. While these figures do not tell the full story of the state of the Church in Australia, and it would be a mistake to use them as the only guide, there is a point, when the rates of reception of the sacraments reaches a level where apprehension is justified. The Church, in the immediate post-conciliar era, was emerging from a time of unprecedented expansion and growth. In that time, indicators such as Mass attendance rates were unusually high. Some downward readjustment could have been anticipated, but this period appears to be over.

As there is no single statistical definition of what constitutes Catholic identity, it is not unreasonable to suggest that those things which the Tradition itself sees as being of critical importance give an accurate guide to the vitality of the community.[18] There can be no question that the Church regards sacraments such as Eucharist and Baptism as foundational.[19] If it is accepted that disassociation from the worshipping community leads to personalised and somewhat benign religious views, then the figures for reception of the sacraments are suggestive of a trend that will see more and more Catholics move away from their origins. Mason and his colleagues have already noted such a clear trend among Generation Y. The alternative view – that religious belief remains reasonably stable in the absence of strong connection with the faith community – seems less plausible.

---

17 Dixon, *Community*, 113.
18 D'Antonio et al., *American*, 27.
19 See, for example, *Code of Canon Law 1983*, 867, 868, 1247, obtained on 10/10/2007 from http://www.vatican.va/ archive/ENG1104/_INDEX.HTM,

It can be argued that a truer indicator of Catholic identity is an interiorisation of belief matched with living a moral life that is animated by Gospel or Kingdom values. Following this argument, whilst practices such as Mass attendance may be on the decline, this is not a measure of the vitality of religious life, but merely of its external manifestation. If externals are, however, too heavily discounted, concepts such as Gospel values are of pivotal importance because adherence to these becomes the key marker of Catholic identity, the boundary between the Church and the world. The problem here is how to distinguish Catholics marked by holding certain values from others in the wider community. This difficulty seems to be particularly acute when dealing with Catholic youth and young adults.[20] If a group has no or very low boundaries or distinguishing features, then it loses sociological validity. The author is unaware of any study that shows that Catholics, taken as an undifferentiated whole, display different values than other groups, once factors such as socio-economic background have been controlled for.[21] On a conceptual level, it is hard to see why they should. The search for a set of values that distinguishes Catholics from others is also based on an assumption that these values define all Catholics. But Greeley himself has remarked:

> Every generalisation about values that begins with the word Catholic is likely to be misleading, if not erroneous, precisely because the generalisation will mask substantial differences in values that exist among Catholic subpopulations.[22]

---

20 Leslie J. Francis, 'Catholic Schools and Catholic Values? A Study of Moral and Religious Values Among 13-15 Year Old Pupils Attending Non-Denominational and Catholic Schools in England and Wales', *International Journal of Education and Religion*, 2002, 3(1), 69-81.
21 Dixon, *Community*, 75.
22 Greeley, *Social Portrait*, 252.

The Catholic imagination?

In his analysis of the Church in America, Greeley acknowledged the sharp declines in both Mass attendance and personal prayer.[23] He does not see these as relatively significant, and places much value on what he terms the ongoing strength of the Catholic imagination, which he argued is qualitatively different from a Protestant imagination.[24] A detailed study of Catholic imagination will not be undertaken here; however, the key relevant question has to do with the durability of such imagination. Is this imagination somehow more resilient than Catholic beliefs and practices? Greeley stated that "the uniquely Catholic heritage, views of God and their world, and the relationship between the two continue to be durable – unchanged and probably unchangeable."[25] Imagination, however, can only be passed on and cultivated if it is nurtured and exercised.[26]

A number of American researchers have provided a different perspective on the vitality of the Church in the United States. Commenting on the generational differences amongst American Catholics, D'Antonio and his colleagues have noted much less commitment among the millennial generation. They comment: "If a sizeable number of young adults do not understand their faith well enough to explain it to their own children, they have a problem, and so does the Church."[27] Concentrating on youth, Smith and Denton noted the religious laxity of American Catholic teenagers. They offered a variety of explanations for this but none of these are indicative of a community that is not facing significant challenges.[28]

23 Greeley, *Religion*, 1.
24 Greeley, *Catholic Imagination*, esp. 1-77.
25 Greeley, *Imagination*, 186.
26 Greeley does acknowledge the need for the cultivation of the Catholic imagination. See Greeley, *Catholic Imagination*, 131-137.
27 D'Antonio at al., *Americans Catholics Today*, 83.
28 Smith and Denton, *Soul*, 193-217.

They concluded:

> Compared both to official Church norms of faithfulness and to other types of Christian teens in the United States, contemporary U.S. Catholic teens are faring rather badly. On most measures of religious faith, belief, experience, and practice, Catholic teens as a whole show up as fairly weak.[29]

In light of what has been presented here, the argument can be made that the new evangelisation cannot be described as unnecessary. Views about the urgency of the task may vary but the basic premise is sound.

Nevertheless, some have argued that the new evangelisation is not required because a general spiritual awareness is replacing religious belief and commitment. In this view, the widespread mantra, "I'm spiritual but not religious!" may not be a cause for concern but of reassurance. Spirituality can be conceived of in a number of ways. In an excellent discussion of this issue, Mason and his colleagues point out the need for clear definitions of spirituality so that dialogue can be purposeful.[30] This is especially important in a discussion about the relationship between spirituality and religious commitment. If we take spirituality to mean a highly privatised, personal, and idiosyncratic set of beliefs that do not have a clear derivation from a faith tradition, are not expressed in a communal and ritualistic way, and do not have a strong impact on one's way of life, then the rise of this spirituality should pose a serious concern to Catholic leaders. Described in this way, spirituality seems to have a number of parallels with the loose affiliation of many Catholics today. To point out that large numbers of Catholics have this spirituality is merely to restate the problem of low commitment in a different manner. It leaves the question of how to respond unanswered.

---

29 Smith and Denton, *Soul*, 216.
30 Mason est al., *Generation Y*, 33-42.

If we take spirituality in its more classical sense of an intense personal encounter with the Divine leading to a transformation of life, and all of this being closely connected with a great Tradition, then spirituality is almost the natural ally of those who are trying to promote stronger religious commitment. However, Mason and his colleagues noted that it is the first, more diffuse type of spirituality that appears to be on the ascent amongst many young people today, even though they themselves find it hard to articulate.[31]

In summary, if large numbers of Catholics see themselves as spiritual in the first sense of the term, then the problems facing the Church are twofold. First, this kind of spirituality runs counter to the whole Catholic metaphysic, which sees the individual in communion with God through the Church. To suggest, as Tacey does, that a way forward for Catholics is a "personal and mystical encounter" between the believer and God is to undermine not just the ecclesiology of communion but also any sense of the Church as the Mystical Body of Christ.[32] The basis of the Christian life is the ongoing fellowship with God and with others expressed most perfectly in the celebration of the Eucharist. If a person claims to be a Catholic but rejects this communal understanding of faith in favour of a private, personal, and eclectic set of beliefs and practices, then there is a serious rupture between the views of the individual and the Tradition. Guardini noted one implication of this view:

> The way to the truth then cannot be to "seek God" as we like to say merely through our own experiences and our own thoughts. For if the seeker pictures God in this way and establishes a relationship with him, he really remains with himself – only in a more subtle and more closed binding manner than if he declared openly, "I do not want anything to do with God; I am sufficient for myself."[33]

On a more sociological level, to recast many Catholics today as

31 Mason et al., *Generation Y*, 38.
32 Tacey, *Spirituality Revolution*, 169.
33 Guardini, *Church of the Lord*, 60-61.

(diffusely) spiritual rather than having a low level of commitment does nothing to address the rationale for the new evangelisation, namely, that any organisation or group that does not have a critical mass of individuals who are able to participate fully in its life and work faces serious challenges.

Many Catholic agencies face a problematic future if their ranks are filled with those who express this diffuse spirituality. This kind of low level commitment has many similarities with the religious allegiance described previously as requiring very little of its adherents, giving them a wide range of choices, allowing them to retain existing social networks, freeing then them from an existential void, and giving some small degree of fellowship with many others like them. These adherents are allowed to be religious but in a very limited, secular, and privatised sense. In terms of vicarious religion, they have not removed the safety net from their lives.

The question remains, however, how is this group to be evangelised? If this spirituality becomes the default position of many Catholics, it almost stands in the way of the conversion that Pope John Paul II envisaged, a profound re-orientation of life and an encounter with Christ. Emile Griffin describes this type of conversion as "the discovery, made gradually or suddenly, that God is real. It is the perception that this real God loves us personally and acts mercifully and justly towards each of us. Conversion is the direct experience of the saving power of God."[34] If spirituality is not rooted in this sense of searching for the Divine, it runs the risk of being an impediment to the new evangelisation.

---

34 Emile Griffin, *Turning: Reflections on the Experience of Conversion.* (New York: Doubleday, 1980), 15.

Polarisation of the Church?

A brief typology

Richard Gaillardetz remarked that, in his experience of university students in the United States, it was possible to make a distinction between two groups of students.[35] On the one hand, the majority had a diminished sense of Catholic identity. On the other hand, there was a much smaller group that had a very strong interest in what it means to be a Catholic.[36] This phenomenon has been noted in the wider literature. Fulton and his colleagues described this committed group of young adult Catholics as *"Core Catholic,"* distinguished by their involvement in wider Catholic networks such as parishes, and their readiness to identify themselves as Catholic.[37]

In their classification of young adult Catholics, Hoge and his colleagues used similar terminology to describe two kinds of religious expression: *"Church as Choice Catholic"* and *"Core Catholic."*[38] Core Catholics were described as the ten percent of their sample who had a less individualistic approach to religious belief and practice, took seriously papal teaching (even if they disagreed with it), prayed daily and regarded weekly Mass attendance as a key marker of Catholic identity. Smith and Denton reported a similar figure, ten percent, for young American Catholics who identified their religion as being extremely important in shaping their daily lives. By comparison the figure for mainline Protestants was 20% and 29% for conservative

---

35 For a cautionary note about the use of labels see, Cathleen Kaveny, 'Young Catholics: When Labels Don't Fit', *Commonweal*, 2004, 131, November 19, 19-21.

36 Richard Gaillardetz, 'Apologetics, Evangelisation and Ecumenism Today', *Origins* 35/1 (2005), 9.

37 John Fulton, Anthony Abela, Irena Borowik, Teresa Dowling, Penny Marler and Luigi Tomasi, *Young Catholics at the New Millennium; The Religion and Morality of Young Adults in Western Countries.* (Dublin: University College Press, 2000), esp. 9-13.

38 Hoge et al., *Young Adult Catholics*, esp. 47-54.

Protestants.[39] Colleen Carroll coined the term *"New Faithful"* to describe a tendency among some young adult Christians to identify strongly with traditional religious positions.[40] David Whalen used the term "contemporary traditionals" to describe a similar group, although this group did not accept all Church teachings, a characteristic of the new faithful.[41] William Portier identified a group among university students which he called evangelical Catholics, who sought to better understand their faith and desired to share it with others.[42] Rymarz and Graham found amongst some Catholic adolescents a strong familial pattern of religious belief and practice. This can be described as a tendency to closely identify with the beliefs of parents as opposed to more typical communitarian or less committed modes of religious expression.[43]

Dealing with younger Catholics

It would appear that some young Catholics have avoided what Kay and Francis call the "drift from the Churches."[44] How then should this group be viewed against the broader template of contemporary Catholicism and the new evangelisation? Speaking for many, Rausch articulated well a concern about the impact of this "significant minority" of young Catholics:

> The energy and commitment of these young Catholics is an encouraging sign. Still their potential to advance the Church's mission will be lost if they prove unable to move beyond an

---

39 Smith and Denton, *Soul*, 37-53.
40 Colleen Carroll, *The New Faithful: Why Young Faithful are Embracing Christian Orthodoxy.* (Chicago: Loyola Press, 2004).
41 David M. Whalen, 'The Emergence of the Contemporary Traditionalist', *Review for Religious*, 61 November-December 2002, 585-593.
42 William L. Portier, 'Here Come the Catholic Evangelicals', *Communio*, 2004, 31, 50-59, at 52-53.
43 Rymarz and Graham, *Drifting*.
44 William Kay and Leslie Francis. *Drift from the Churches: Attitude toward Christianity during Childhood and Adolescence.* (Cardiff: University of Wales Press, 1996).

uncritical triumphalism or retreat into a new Catholic ghetto. A restoration of the pre-Vatican II sub-culture is neither possible nor desirable. They need to find common ground with the larger group of young Catholics and with the mainstream Church if they are to realise an authentic catholicity and truly serve the Church.[45]

In light of previous chapters, a number of points can be made which address the concerns articulated by Rausch. First, a characteristic of contemporary Catholicism is the lack of religious socialisation of young Catholics. This can be contrasted with earlier eras where socialisation was very evident and, perhaps, unreflective. There is no question that the Catholic world of the third millennium, in countries such as Australia, is very different from the cultural expressions that were dominant over fifty years ago. Indeed, many of the underlying attitudes that shaped pre-conciliar Catholicism are almost unimaginable to Catholics today. An appropriate metaphor for the impact of the Council is *revolution*.[46] One of the characteristics of revolutions is that they change underlying structures and cannot be undone – so there is no going back to earlier forms, no matter how ardent the desire to do so. Those who wish to recreate a bygone world have no sense of the movement of history, and cannot make much of a contribution to the discussion on the future of the Church. To disregard the past as if it has nothing to offer us is, however, an equally myopic position. A necessary but intellectually difficult debate is how to articulate an intermediate position.

In terms of the engagement with culture, the Church has not yet achieved the active discernment of cultural dispositions as posited by Gallagher. This is an intermediary position between innocent acceptance and hostility toward culture.[47] Those who

---

45 Rausch, *Culture of Choice*, 117.
46 Greeley, *Catholic Revolution*.
47 Gallagher, *Clashing Symbols*, 118-121.

express a concern about a return to pre-Vatican II mentality need to acknowledge that some young Catholics, in an environment where there is little opportunity to express Catholic identity, need to have their uncharacteristically strong religious beliefs and practices affirmed. This is not a return to a pre-conciliar worldview but, more aptly, a response to a very different social reality, one that is hardly comparable to the 1950s. For some, participation in the Catholic subculture of the pre-conciliar era may have been an external, social phenomenon with little personal significance. In contemporary culture, however, a Catholic who wishes to participate more fully in, say, the sacramental life of the Church is most likely choosing to do so on the basis of conviction and belief. The fact that most other Catholics do not do this does not invalidate their choice.

This raises a deeper issue here about how the contemporary Church deals with those individuals who, to use the title of Rausch's book, choose to be "Catholic in a culture of choice."[48] The present author has argued that if we follow a communitarian model, characterised by low conflict with wider culture, low sociological boundaries, and high levels of inclusion, the Church is relatively successful in dealing with youth and young adults. If, however, a commitment model is followed, typified by strong interest in the tradition, powerful affective experiences, and high boundaries, the Church is less successful.[49] Those who fit into a communitarian sense of Church do not generally provide much challenge or conflict. They are, in the main, very content with their current position, which could be described as low cost with high benefit. The Church, by providing a range of services, such as

---

48 Writing in the early 1980s Dulles also raises this issue. "For some reason the Catholic Church seems unable to capitalize on the yearnings for religious commitment and spiritual experiences felt by so many of our contemporaries." Avery Dulles, *A Church to Believe In: Discipleship and the Dynamics of Freedom.* (New York: Crossroads, 1982), 3.
49 Rymarz, *Communitarian,* 57.

educational institutions and an overarching but somewhat distant narrative, meets the needs of these Catholics very well. The situation of those who are committed, or who seek to be, is more problematic.

A key question is what does the Church do to assist younger Catholics who wish to strengthen their faith commitment above conventional levels? Does the Church meet the needs of those who want to express their faith in a supportive environment, want to have contact with others who share their views, want, on occasion, to be in a place where they are not in the minority, who would like to have some of their questions answered, who want to take part in uplifting and dignified worship, or want help in rejecting cultural pressures and influences that envelop them? Labelling those individuals as outside the mainstream may not be helpful. The challenge for all Catholic schools in particular, irrespective of sub-grouping or label, is to provide some type of formation and support program which addresses the needs and concerns of those who have chosen to be Catholic in the third millennium.[50] To return to the analogy of the religious consumer, it is reasonable to assume that those individuals will be more demanding than their more typical Catholic peers and this may place some strain on existing structures. Bouma expressed both the challenge and the potential of this new type of religious consumer when he wrote:

> A cohort of religiously articulate young people … have a much more developed sense of their spirituality than previous generations. They will be more demanding and sophisticated consumers in the religious marketplace. The religious organisations that rise to this challenge will grow; those that keep insulting their market – as is the case for much of what passes for mainstream Christianity – will not.[51]

50 Richard M. Rymarz, 'Reform, Conservative and Neo-Orthodox-Distinctions in Contemporary Judaism: A Useful Lexicon for Catholics?' *Australasian Catholic Record*, 2002, 79 (1), 18-30.
51 Bouma, *Australian Soul*, 208.

Many modern institutional structures took shape in an era when religious socialisation of Catholics and the interconnection of home, parish, and family were strong. These conditions no longer exist, and so new structures will form. In the future, the Catholic community will be smaller, reflecting the movement from a Church of obligation to a Church of personal conviction. This will occur not as a matter of policy but as a consequence of the chains that bind many to the Catholic Tradition becoming weaker and weaker.[52] In the future, very few Catholics will be part of Church groups because of religious socialisation or societal pressure. One example of this is the composition of Catholic student groups at tertiary institutions. It is unlikely that anyone joining these groups now does so because it is something their parents did or because they are following the majority of their schoolmates. It can be assumed that those who approach these groups will be in a distinct minority, but do so out of a serious interest in learning more about and strengthening their faith. This is not a mandate for these groups to become ideological or partisan but it does require the wider Church to have something positive to offer on the basis that those who express interest are genuine. Consideration could be given to providing specialised pastoral ministry to active Catholic youth, a point that will be elaborated on in Chapter 5.

The faithful remnant?

Some have noted that this type of argument is consistent with a "faithful remnant" view of the Church.[53] In this view, a few 'hang on' in spite of the overwhelmingly secular nature of the surrounding

---

52 Ernest Troeltsch, *The Social Teaching of the Christian Churches, vol 1.* (London: George Allen and Unwin, 1931).
53 Jason Byassee, 'Being Benedict; The Pope's First Year', *Christian Century*, 2006, April 18, 2-8. Douglas J. Hall, *The Future of the Church.* (Toronto: United Church Publishing House, 1989).

culture, exclude others, and turn their attention inwards, manifesting a type of Catholic quietism, focusing on personal piety rather than engagement with others.[54] However, the problem facing the Church in the short to medium term is not exclusion. Rather, there appear to be few compelling reasons for loosely affiliated people to strengthen their commitment, and so many drift away.[55] The predicament the Church faces is a widespread and resolute lack of interest in strengthening religious commitment. The figures for reception of sacraments, for example, bear this out. As Dixon pointed out, the figures for reception of the sacrament of marriage amongst Catholics is falling quite dramatically and now appears to be the exception rather than the norm.

Kavanaugh goes as far as to link Catholic marriage and celibacy as two radically counter-cultural choices.[56] Unlike the sacraments of initiation and confirmation, marriage typically occurs well after school years. Those who wish to marry in a Catholic service cannot be carried along by the crowd, as often happens at, say, confirmation.[57] They need to make a deliberate, adult decision to be involved. The issue is not whether people are being excluded but, to reiterate and recast an earlier question, why should a couple choose to marry in a Catholic service? Given that the power of familial tradition is weakening and will continue to do so, what other reasons would make this decision plausible? Or, more starkly, what does the Church in general and the Catholic school in particular, offer the religious consumer?

---

54 Paul VI addresses this concern directly, see EN, 31. Religious youth tend to be the most socially committed. This finding should allay the fears of those who tend to see religious commitment as taking the place of social involvement. Mason et al. *Generation Y*, esp. 137-151.
55 Portier, *Catholic Evangelicals*, 62-63.
56 Kavanaugh, *Following Christ*, 163-168.
57 E. Thomas Lawson and Robert N. McCauley, *Rethinking Religion: Connecting Cognition and Culture.* (Cambridge: Cambridge University Press, 1990), esp. 31-41, 60-77.

Most young adult Catholics are content with their current, relatively loose affiliation and see no reason to increase their level of commitment. The social networks that they move in largely eschew religious fellowship of any serious nature. Attempts to recruit them to faith based organisations are often fruitless. D'Antonio and Pogorelic, for example, in their analysis of the *Voice of the Faithful* (VOTF) movement in the United States noted that the demographic profile of membership is heavily slanted to those well over the age of fifty.[38] Few Generation X or Generation Y Catholics are members. They note that VOTF is a liberal, reform-minded group. It would be a mistake to see the lack of interest of younger people in groups like VOTF as a reflection on that organisation alone. It is indicative of a more general trend that underlines the difficulty inherent in the new evangelisation. Youth and young adults are scarce in many Catholic organisations. The fundamental question is how can this be rectified?

Maintaining a remnant is also not a position that is consistent with the new evangelisation.[59] In the first instance people are unlikely to join a group they see as surviving only as a historical rump of something that was once much greater. The whole thrust of the new evangelisation is outward toward the wider culture, to try to bring Christ to people as well as to the society in which Catholics find themselves. Its aim is outreach not exclusion and changing not just individuals but also cultures. Finally, the idea that people, especially younger ones, who show high levels of religious commitment, are not interested in getting involved in wider issues such as social justice is mistaken. Mason and his colleagues have shown that while it is true that many of Generation Y are not interested in social outreach,

---

58 William D'Antonio and Anthony Pogorelic, *Voices of the Faithful: Loyal Catholics Striving for Change.* (New York: Crossroads, 2007), 67-90.
59 James Hunter, *American Evangelicalism: Conservative Religion and the Quandary of Modernity.* (New Brunswick, NJ: Rutgers University Press, 1983).

those who are interested are much more likely to also report high
levels of religious commitment of the traditional variety.[60]

To summarise: having a clear message, the promise of involvement
in loving communities, and forming lasting, significant human
relationships may persuade those on the periphery to associate at a
deeper level. This is especially so if they see the Church as having
something to offer that they cannot get somewhere else. People who
choose to remain or become members will be comfortable with a
community where they can practise what it means to be a Catholic
– to be part of this conversation. Being Catholic will become more
counter cultural, but also more descriptive because the label will bring
with it more characteristic beliefs and practices which befit a group
that has established sufficient boundaries around itself to distinguish
it from the wider culture. In recent history, perhaps no one has
been more influential in establishing a positive and dynamic view
on the intersection between culture and the Church than Romano
Guardini. Yet, he acknowledged that this exchange is not one-sided
and uncritical. Robert Krieg noted, "Guardini was aware, too, that the
Christian faith must at times be critical of a specific culture in which it
exists."[61] What is needed is a sense of balance and strong self-identity.

The Spectre of Fundamentalism

The Council urged Catholics to reexamine all aspects of their lives,
both on a personal and institutional level. One result of this process
was the Church becoming less proclamatory and more dialogical.
Is then a reemphasis on the evangelising nature of the Church a
return to the triumphalism of the 1950s, a simplistic and uncritical

---

60 Mason et al., *Generation Y*, 127.
61 Robert A. Krieg, 'A Precursor's Life and Work' in Robert A. Krieg (Ed), *Romano Guardini: Proclaiming the Sacred in a Modern World*. (Chicago: Liturgy Training Publications, 1995), 36.

Catholicism? The new evangelisation is undoubtedly a proclamation. It requires, therefore, at the least a certain confidence in the message that is being proclaimed. This is not a simplistic attitude but one which resonates with the experience of the first Christians. There is a directness and encapsulation about this but this need not be seen as reversion to outdated concepts. What often sidetracks this discussion is the incorrect and indiscriminate use of terms such as fundamentalist.[62] Two ways in which this term can be incorrectly applied to the new evangelisation will be described here.

Firstly, there is the sense that the new evangelisation represents some type of overly simplistic rendering of the tradition and does not do justice to the richness of Catholicism. To have clear convictions, however, based on substantial teaching, and to be prepared to argue for these is not fundamentalism, but more properly described as a Christian characteristic.[63] Ratzinger, in a well-known homily, outlined some of the problems inherent in using the term fundamentalist to describe Catholics:

> Having a clear faith, based on the Creed of the Church, is often labelled today as a fundamentalism. Whereas, relativism, which is letting oneself be tossed and "swept along by every wind of teaching", looks like the only attitude (acceptable) to today's standards. We are moving towards a dictatorship of relativism which does not recognise anything as for certain and which has as its highest goal one's own ego and one's own desires.[64]

What is needed here are careful distinctions that can differentiate,

---

62 For a fuller discussion of so-called Catholic fundamentalism see, Richard M. Rymarz, 'Is Fundamentalism a Useful Descriptor of Trends in Contemporary Catholicism?' *Australasian Catholic Record*, 2007, 84 (1), 56-67.

63 Compare with Michael Trainor, 'On the Rise Again: Neo Fundamentalism in Australian Catholicism', Part One, *Compass*, 2004, 9–13. Michael Trainor, 'On the Rise Again: Neo Fundamentalism in Australian Catholicism', Part Three, *Compass*, 2005, 33–39.

64 Obtained from http://www.vatican.va/gpII/documents/homily-pro-eligendo-pontifice_20050418_it.html, 4/5/05.

on the one hand, between acceptance of key beliefs, and on the other, between a variety of approaches as to how the Church should interact with the wider culture. Such distinctions are much more common in the sociological analysis of Jewish groups, who are generally more practised at making careful distinctions. Heilman and Cohen, for example, note that a Jew who believes that God not only exists, but created an ordered universe, that the Torah was revealed by God to Moses on Mt Sinai and that the Messiah will come, is correctly described as an Orthodox believer, not a Jewish fundamentalist. How they react to the world can further be characterised as a parochial or cosmopolitism acculturation.[65]

In a similar vein, if a person accepts the evangelical nature of the Church as set out in the documents of Vatican II, has a strong personal commitment to Christ, who expresses their faith within an ecclesial community, and who wishes to proclaim this to others, he or she is not a Catholic fundamentalist. They are operating well within the parameters of valid debate and discourse. When the term fundamentalist is used, it is often not referring back to a formal definition but, with further elaboration, has some similarity to conservatism.[66] Even the term, "conservative", used as a descriptor of the new evangelisation, is contentious because it fails to take into account the developments in missiology and ecclesiology from which it arose.

Secondly, there is the sense that the new evangelisation is a retreat from the modern world and its complexity, and in some ways a disavowal of Vatican II. The new evangelisation is seen by John Paul II as having its origins at the Council, "the new evangelisation which originated precisely at the Second Vatican Council."[67]

---

65 Samuel Heilman and Steven Cohen, *Cosmopolitans &Parochials: Modern Orthodox Jews in America.* (Chicago: University of Chicago Press, 1989).
66 Patrick Arnold, 'The Rise of Catholic Fundamentalism', *America,* April 1, 1987, 297.
67 John Paul II, *Threshold,* 160.

So those who try to see ways to implement it cannot be described as rejecting outright the teachings of the Council.[68] One of the most pressing theological issues in the immediate future for Catholics is how the teachings of the Council have been interpreted and promulgated.[69] This complex issue cannot be addressed explicitly here, suffice it to say that it seems reasonable for Catholics in times of turmoil and disputation to use the teaching of popes and bishops in union with them as a reliable guide. This is not papocentrisim but merely a reflection of the basic Catholic principle of seeing the pope as the centre of unity. This line of argument seems to have at least as much credibility, in a historico-theological sense, as a contrasting view which sees the recent popes as somehow subverting an ecumenical council. This alternate perspective is well put by Ludwig: "The Council's vision found a formidable opponent in the election of the charismatic Karol Wojtyla as John Paul II. His conservative leadership put Vatican II in a deep freeze."[70] Ludwig goes on to describe a "gulf" between the Church's hierarchy and, amongst others, "dedicated Catholic believers."[71] This type of view is very difficult to reconcile with the goals of the new evangelisation, as bishops and laity are set against each other by it.[72]

Neither is the new evangelisation a manifestation of what Trainor

---

68 William Dinges and James Hitchcock, 'Roman Catholic Traditionalism and Activist Conservatism in the United States,' in Martin Marty and E. Scot Appleby, (Eds), *Fundamentalism Observed.* (Chicago, University of Chicago Press, 1991), esp. 77-82.

69 A useful starting point for this discussion is De Lubac's classic contrast between the authentic Council and the *para Council* – the interpretation of the Second Vatican Council that became imbedded in contemporary Catholic culture. Henri de Lubac, *A Brief Catechesis on Nature and Grace.* (San Francisco: Ignatius Press, 1984), 235–260. For a contrasting view see Paul Collins, *Papal Power: A Proposal for Change in Catholicism's Third Millennium.* (London: Fount, 1997), 97-125.

70 Robert A. Ludwig, *Reconstructing Catholicism for a New Generation,* (New York: Crossroad, 1996), 32.

71 Ludwig, *Reconstructing,* 32-33.

72 Donovan, *Distinctively Catholic,* 175-177.

typifies as "nostalgia for earlier expressions of Catholicism" and
as demonstrating selectivity about what parts of contemporary
culture should be acknowledged.[73] Almond and his colleagues
describe selectivity as a three-fold phenomenon which illustrates the
relationship between the believer and modernity.[74] There are some
elements of the modern world that can be readily accepted and
assimilated, and others rejected. Fundamentalists closely scrutinise
those parts of the modern world they are prepared to accept and
are generally more comfortable in a tightly controlled world of their
own construction. All religious groups, however, are selective in the
sense that all regulate how their community integrates with the wider
culture. The culture of a community such as the Catholic Church, with
ancient roots and a desire to live out the hermeneutic of continuity,
has a range that surpasses any particular culture at any time.

It is necessary, therefore, that some parts of the tradition
be stressed at any time as opposed to other aspects. The new
evangelisation is one manifestation of a change in emphasis. If this is
not done periodically, then the Church would never adapt to changing
historical realties.[75] There is often a bias in any organisation to stress
those parts of their heritage which define an identity, which create
a boundary.[76] If boundaries are not in place, and maintained, then
there is little difference between religious communities and others in
the wider culture.[77]

73 Michael Trainor, 'On the Rise Again: Neo Fundamentalism in Australian Catholicism,
Part Two', *Compass*, 2004, 33.
74 Gabriel Almond, Emmanuel Sivan and. R. Scott Appleby, 'Fundamentalism: Genus
and Species' in Marty Martin and R. Scott Appleby (Eds), *Fundamentalisms Comprehended*,
(Chicago: University of Chicago Press, 1995), 406.
75 Joseph Ratzinger, *Principles of Catholic Theology: Building Stones for a Fundamental Theology*,
(San Francisco: Ignatius Press, 1987), 393.
76 Hoge et al., *Young Adult Catholics*, 107–149.
77 Donna Freitas, *Sex and the Soul: Juggling Sexuality, Spirituality, Romance and Religion on
American College Campuses*, (New York: Oxford University Press, 2008).

The critical issue is what boundaries are established and maintained; in other words, how these are selected, not that selection has taken place. Proper boundaries need to reflect the core beliefs of the tradition that are of pivotal historical and ongoing importance, and are not constructed to react to transitory circumstances. A case could be made for some boundaries being unnecessary because they represent tangential elements in the tradition. The new evangelisation is centred on the concept that the Church is by its very nature evangelical and the Christian life is a radical one based on a close personal relationship with Christ. These concepts, in recent times, have not always been at the forefront of Catholic consciousness. By emphasising them, however, has an invalid or reactionary selection been made? It seems hard to argue for this on theological, and especially on ecclesiological grounds.

The New Evangelisation and Church Reform

Reform before evangelisation?

Richard McBrien put well the view that any type of mission or evangelisation is conditional on Church reform: "To be concerned about the renewal and reform of the Church is to be concerned about mission as well."[78] McBrien's approach, however, may also be seen as one which does not place the highest priority on evangelisation, a view reflected in the new edition of his monumental work, *Catholicism*, published in 1994. In this, there are few references to evangelisation and none to the new evangelisation.[79] In the earlier edition, published in 1980, McBrien sees a danger in narrowing the concept of

---

78 Richard P. McBrien, 'Some Say, "Leave the Church Alone, Get Out There and Evangelise",' *National Catholic Reporter*, 1999, 36, November 12, 21.
79 Avery R. Dulles, 'Evangelising Theology', *First Things*, 1996, March, 61.1, 27-32, at 29.

evangelisation and argues that a more diffuse sense is consistent with Pope Paul VI's thought:

> Some Christians assume a militant posture. They call for renewed efforts of "evangelisation" understood not in the broad and comprehensive manner of Paul VI's 1975 Apostolic Exhortation, *Evangelii Nuntiandi*, – the proclamation of the word, the celebration of the sacraments, the offering of corporate witness to Christ, and anticipation in the struggle for peace and justice – but in the narrow sense of 'making converts' or bringing 'fallen-away' Catholics back to the Church.[80]

This view tends to downplay what Pope Paul VI in *Evangelii Nuntiandi* called, "true evangelisation," namely, its Christocentric core: "There is no true evangelisation if the name, the teachings, the promise, the kingdom and the mystery of Jesus of Nazareth, the Son of God are not proclaimed."[81] This Christocentric focus is reinforced in various contemporary episcopal documents such as the call of Archbishop Wilson, President of the Australian Catholic Bishops Conference, for a Year of Grace made during the *ad limina* visit of Australian bishops to Rome in 2011. The emphasis of this year is described in these terms; "We have decided to call the whole Church in Australia to celebrate A Year of Grace from Pentecost 2012 to Pentecost 2013. Through this time we will seek to contemplate the face of Jesus and to listen to his voice at a new depth, in the belief that only he can lead us into the future, that only he can make us one in faith, in hope, in love."[82]

This emphasis on conversion can be associated with militant

---

80 Richard P. McBrien, *Catholicism, Volume One.* (Oak Grove, MN: Winston Press. 1980), 268.
81 EN, 22.
82 Address of Archbishop Wilson to His Holiness Benedict XVI October 5th 2011 obtained on 21/10/11 from from http://www.cathnews.com/article.aspx?acid=28706

Christianity.[83] This does not reflect the new evangelisation of Pope John Paul II as recorded in the statements of various Episcopal conferences. In 1992 the United States bishops, for example, issued a document *Go Make Disciples*, Goal 2 of which reads:

> To invite all people in the United States, whatever their social or cultural background, to hear the message of salvation in Jesus Christ so they may come to join us in the fullness of the Catholic faith.[84]

McBrien does not specify what conditions are needed before genuine evangelisation can occur but criticised the view put forth by Cardinal Hume that, "a trick of the devil is to divert good people from the task of evangelisation by embroiling them in endless controversial issues."[85] He sees this as creating a false dichotomy between the internal life of the Church and concern for mission. This critique is, however, predicated on an attitude that sees reform as critical or at least as important as evangelisation. This view is hard to reconcile with the ecclesiological vision of the Church as being fundamentally missionary in nature. A distinction, though, needs to be made here between various types of reform based largely on their impact and reform that has a theological basis.

Types of reform

In terms of Church life, there are many reforms that are local and organisational in nature. D'Antonio and Pogorelic, for example, noted that many American Catholics who are members of "Voice of the Faithful" are especially concerned with how bishops deal with

---

83 Vatican Congregation for the Doctrine of the Faith, 'Doctrinal Note on some Aspects of Evangelisation'. Obtained on 14/12/2007 from http://www.usccb.org/comm/archives/2007/07-204.shtml.
84 United States Conference of Catholic Bishops, 'Go ad Make Disciples: A National Plan and Strategy for Catholic Evangelisation in the U.S.', *Origins*, 22, 1992, December 3, 423-432 at 429.
85 McBrien, *Leave*, 21.

cases of clerical sexual abuse and other accountability issues.[86] There is no question that if the Church is to be seen as plausible, then the scandal of sexual abuse must be addressed as a matter of the highest importance. As Robinson commented: "It's hard to imagine a more total contradiction of everything that Jesus Christ stood for, and it would be difficult to overestimate the pervasive and lasting harm it has done to the Church."[87] These concerns can be addressed within a framework that still prioritises mission and evangelisation. If we surmise, however, that proposed reforms involve major theological and juridical issues, this has clear implications for the progress of the new evangelisation. Eric Hodgens, for example, argued that the new evangelisation would not be successful until a series of "roadblocks" were removed.[88] These include challenging much of what has been considered orthodox Catholic theology and moral teaching. The scope of these changes is well captured by his remark that "the new knowledge demands that the Christian message be reformulated in a new catechesis."[89] The new evangelisation, in this view, is restricted until these issues are addressed.[90]

Reform and evangelisation

This view on the primacy of major reform can be further addressed in two ways. The first is historico-theological. The question of further reform of the Church is another manifestation of the wider debate about how the teaching of the Council should be received and implemented. The vision of the new evangelisation provided by

---

86 D'Antonio and Pogorelic, *Voices of the Faithful*, 50-67.
87 Geoffrey Robinson, *Confronting Power and Sex in the Catholic Church: Reclaiming the Spirit of Jesus*. (Mulgrave, Victoria: John Garrett Publishing, 2007), 7.
88 Eric Hodgens, *New Evangelisation in the 21ˢᵗ Century: Removing the Roadblocks*. (Mulgrave, Vic.: John Garrett Publishing, 2008).
89 Hodgens, *21ˢᵗ Century*, 53.
90 Blueprint for Vatican III, *National Catholic Reporter*, 2. Obtained on 7/5/2002 at: www.natcath.com/NCR_Online/archives/050302/050302a.htm.

Pope John Paul II comes out of a particular understanding of the Church in the modern world. This has its roots in *Lumen Gentium* and other conciliar and post-conciliar documents. This vision sees the teaching of the Second Vatican Council as providing a template for a new Pentecost of the Church. It does not see these teachings as being in need of completion or drastic supplementation. To argue for another vision of the Church based on a substantially different interpretation of the Council would lead to different conclusions. To give one example, Dillon saw the Council as, "affirming the equality of membership in the Church of the laity and the ordained as the one 'People of God' and providing Catholics with a rationale for lay emancipatory activism."[91] Given her interpretation, Dillon sees groups such as "Catholics for a Free Choice," who argue that the Church's teaching on abortion needs to be reformed, as a legitimate example of contemporary Catholic pluralism.[92] This group should, therefore, be part of any evangelistic endeavour.

On this premise, the new evangelisation would need to be at least delayed until Church teaching on abortion was changed. Evangelisation in a contemporary context is a difficult task and cannot be effective when attitudes within a tradition on important issues seem irreconcilably conflicted. Religious consumers of the third millennium are not well disposed to sifting through internecine disputes. They are very familiar with this type of scenario in other parts of their lives. Why should they be open to a message and an experience which seems partisan even within the home tradition? This focus here is not on analysing different interpretations of the Council. What is being

---

91 Michelle Dillon, 'Bringing Doctrine Back into Action: The Catholicity of VOTF Catholics and Its Imperative' in William D'Antonio and Anthony Pogorelic, *Voices of the Faithful: Loyal Catholics Striving for Change.* (New York: The Crossroads Publishing Company, 2007), 105-120, at 107.
92 Michelle Dillon, *Catholic Identity: Balancing Reason, Faith and Power.* (New York: Cambridge University Press, 1999), 221-241 at 239.

noted here is that different interpretations of the Council lead to different outcomes, especially as far as evangelisation is concerned.[93]

The second point is sociological. Many of the advocated reforms proceed on the assumptions that if these changes were made many Catholics would be likely to become more strongly committed. This may not be the case. If, however, the conviction is that the reform is necessary on theological or philosophical grounds, it should argued for on this basis, and not on the assumption that it will lead to a reinvigoration of the Church. Many of these proposed reforms can be seen as reducing the cost of religious belief, making being a Catholic easier in contemporary culture.[94] An example that has already been raised is that a majority of Catholics now see the Sunday Mass obligation as not being of critical importance. Following this logic, then, it could be argued that a necessary reform would place less emphasis on weekend Eucharistic worship, despite the Council intending that the Eucharist should occupy an even more central place in the lives of Catholics.

Two comments can be made about this argumentation. First, it would be unwise to disregard any decision about the future of the Church just because it makes the life of Catholics easier.[95] There is, however, substantial literature, discussed earlier, which points to the need for religious groups to retain some sense of tension with the

---

93 Hodgens, for example, dismisses John Paul II's interpretation of Vatican II as "totally reactionary and restorationist." Hodgens, *21ˢᵗ Century*, 20.

94 Thomas C. Reeves, *The Empty Church: Does Organized Religion Matter Anymore?* (New York, Simon & Shuster, 1998), esp. 166-190.

95 Paul VI drew attention to misconstruing the Council as in some way removing burdens from Catholics. "Whoever would see in the Council a weakening of the interior commitments of the Church towards her faith, her traditions, her asceticism, her charity, her spirit of sacrifice, her adherence to the Word and to the cross of Christ, or even an indulgent concession to the fragile and changeable relativistic mentality of world principles and without a transcendent end, or a kind of Christianity that is more permissive and less demanding would be mistaken." Speech to General Chapter of the Salesians, quoted in De Lubac, *Service of the Church*, 368.

wider culture in order to survive. This tension is often marked by obligations placed on believers that do not apply to those who are not members of the group. Some religious groups place significant demands on members and appear to be growing and showing other signs of vigorous internal life. In terms of time, many of these obligations are devoted to the community, and far exceed the hour or so it takes to attend Mass on the weekend. Amongst other things, making these demands gives members a chance to converse with others on what it means to be a part of that community. Finke and Stark have noted that in the recent history of Catholicism, a "worst of both worlds" situation has developed.[96] On the one hand, many of the relatively mild rituals and obligations that Catholics were expected to follow have disappeared or been downgraded. These, taken as a whole, gave the community a sense of identity and cohesion. On the other hand, the most difficult and costly teachings, have, at least in theory, remained. They argue that the Church should re-evaluate its position and place greater stress on the importance of relatively minor obligatory practices.

In summary, it is not obvious how a reform such as placing less emphasis on participation in weekend Eucharistic worship would result in more committed Catholics. One of the features of high levels of commitment is elevated levels of participation. This book is not centred on the legitimacy of Church reform but it can note that many of these may not result in renewal, at least as this is understood in standard sociological terms.

Other reforms may be of more interest to religious professionals rather than more typical Catholics. Cardinal Thomas Winning put this view well:

I do not believe that the structures of the Roman curia are a

---

96 Finke and Stark, *Churching*, 172-181.

> burning issue to the ordinary men and women trying to live out their Catholic faith in the world. Of far greater impact on the lives of most Catholics are the strengths and weaknesses of the local church, both in terms of spiritual leadership and the faith commitment of the laity.[97]

There seems to be some sense in this view. It could be argued that Winning, a former Cardinal Archbishop of Glasgow, had an interest in taking attention away from internal Church debate. It could also be argued that this view reflects those of a person with sound pastoral experience and, to repeat the point, it is not obvious how an issue such as reform of the Roman curia would increase the fervour and commitment of Catholics in Scotland. Leaving aside whether or not it is necessary or urgent, the critical question seems to be: should evangelisation be deferred until curial reform tales place or to some other point in the future?[98]

Concluding Comments

Like any concept, the new evangelisation can be placed under legitimate critical scrutiny. The points raised in this chapter help solidify the notion of the new evangelisation. The need for the new evangelisation arises out of a sense that the Church in countries such as Australia faces important challenges that call for a proportionate response. This is a realistic assessment. What is called for here is discernment and a vision for a way forward. Of special interest here are the ramifications of the new evangelisation for Catholic schools. Certainly not all proposals will be meritorious, but what the new evangelisation allows for is a discussion of some new ways of

---

97 Cardinal Thomas Winning quoted in Horwood, *Future*, 34.
98 This view is powerfully put by Robinson: "Of what use is it to proclaim a 'new evangelisation' to others if we are not seen to have confronted the suppurating ulcer on our body?" Geoffrey Robinson, 'Confront Abuse Don't Manage it', *Eureka Street*, October 2007. Obtained on 10/3/2008 at: http://www.eurekastreet.com.au/article.aspx?acid=3413.

engaging the world, and also of how the Church initiates pastoral outreach. This is an active program and, as such, will not always be fruitful or uncontentious. As an alternative, a more passive stance would probably lead to less reaction but runs the risk of not engaging the wider culture or recognising the historic circumstances in which the Church finds itself. The new evangelisation is rooted in the Christian hope that the Church is incarnational, existing in time and space, and that it can respond to changing circumstances, and be true to its calling to make Christ known throughout the world.

The new evangelisation, like all emerging ideas, needs to be given some space in which to develop and mature. It may signal the emergence of the Church from the fluidity of the immediate post-conciliar era, where there was a certain timidity in taking a strong position on a range of issues. In the tumult of the times this was an understandable response. Any enduring institution, however, cannot profitably remain in an inward-looking state for an indefinite period of time. What is needed is a fair appraisal of what lies ahead and a commitment to a course of action. In countries such as Australia a critical issue is the absence of large numbers of committed younger Catholics. Addressing this needs to be seen as a priority. Other issues such as reform of Church structures are valid and can still be considered within the context of the new evangelisation. It is not proposed here that reform be sidelined. Indeed, a vigorous espousal of the new evangelisation will inevitably lead to new structures emerging in the Church. To put reform ahead of evangelisation, however, is to misread both the signs of the times and to misunderstand the fundamental evangelic identity of the Church.

We are now in a position to move to address directly some of the challenges and issues the new evangelisation poses for Catholic schools. The response contained in the next Chapter is necessarily the fruit of our discursive analysis of the new evangelisation thus far.

5

Some Principles of the New Evangelisation for Catholic Schools

We can better understand the profound meaning of the expression and its inherent appeal by turning to Pope John Paul II, who greatly supported and propagated this idea. He insisted that a "new evangelisation" means "to rekindle in ourselves the impetus of the Church's beginnings and allow ourselves to be filled with the ardour of the apostolic preaching which followed Pentecost. We must revive in ourselves the burning conviction of Paul, who cried out: "Woe to me if I do not preach the Gospel" (*1 Cor* 9:16). This passion will not fail to stir in the Church a new sense of mission, which cannot be left to a group of 'specialists' but must involve the responsibility of all the members of the People of God.[1]

Some Guiding Factors

The quote above from the preparatory document for the XIIIth Synod of Bishops to be held in 2012 captures well the ardour that the new evangelisation both requires and inspires. The new evangelisation as envisaged by John Paul II is a bold strategy in as much as it sets a clear benchmark for success. Its goal is nothing less than the personal conversion of those who have lost an active sense of what it means to be a disciple of Jesus. By focusing on such personal and challenging goals, the new evangelisation signifies a shift away from the more passive sense of the interaction between the Church and culture that was prevalent in the post-conciliar period. Disciples of Christ are likely to engage in the prevailing culture in countries such

1 *XIII Synod of Bishops, Lineamenta: The New Evangelisation for the Transmission of the Christitan Faith* obtained 1/10/11 from http://www.vatican.va/roman_curia/synod/documents/rc_synod_doc_20110202_lineamenta-xiii-assembly_en.html

as Australia in a critical fashion that places more emphasis on the distinct and counter cultural aspects of the Christian message. Any high-stakes strategy runs the risk of not succeeding, at least not everywhere. Indeed George Weigel, noting the legacy of John Paul II, comments that despite his best efforts, at least in its initial stages, the new evangelisation of Europe has floundered: "No pope since the Middle Ages had tried harder to arouse Europe's Christian spirit. The response, to be charitable, was tepid".[2] Indeed the task of the new evangelisation in schools requires a consistent and concerted effort, akin to restoring Venice from the insidious creep of the Adriatic – a metaphor used by White.[3] The new evangelisation brings with it as well, all the difficulties that face a new approach or paradigm. However, just as Paul's endeavours at the Areopagus may not have been seen as an immediate success, Paul could do no other so inflamed was he by the desire to evangelise.

The Church too understood, as an agent of evangelisation not by choice but by its very nature, must carry on its Pauline mission with an eye to more long-term goals and not be discouraged by what seems to be failure. The commitment to the new evangelisation needs to be consistent, realising that the task ahead is difficult, that it can be mitigated by intelligence and resourcefulness. As Lonergan remarks, "Ours is a new age, and enormous tasks lie ahead. But we shall be all the more likely to surmount them, if we take the trouble to understand what is going forward and why".[4] Indeed the search for principles of the new evangelisation that can be used in schools can be seen as part of a much wider movement that seeks to provide

---

2 George Weigel, *God's Choice: Pope Benedict XVI and the Future of the Catholic Church*. (New York: HarperCollins, 2005), 57.

3 Dan White, 'Restoring Venice: A Call to the New Evangelisation', in Anne Benjamin and Dan Riley, (Eds), *Catholic Schools: Hope in Uncertain Times*. (Mulgrave, Vic.: John Garratt Publishing, 2008), 79-191 at 187.

4 Lonergan, *Future*, 163.

leadership and direction to youth and young adults in a culture which often leaves them dangerously vulnerable. Smith and his colleagues, for instance, see religious groups as being well situated to assist young to adults move into a more grounded, morally sophisticated position, one that moves beyond the individualism and consumerism that our culture seems fixated on.

> Religious communities can play a role in all of this. Many emerging adults once belonged to communities of faith in younger years, where they presumably enjoyed the benefits of community, instruction in their faith, and moral teaching. Many religious congregations in fact devote significant resources to children and teenagers, yet unfortunately seem to passively accept that their life ties to youth will be lost after high school. But this need not happen.[5]

For the new evangelisation to have a successful expression in Catholic schools, the interaction between the Church and the wider culture must be viewed as a dynamic, but not discontinuous, process. In this view it is legitimate to describe ebbs and flows in the vitality of the Church, and by coloration, Catholic schools. In countries such as Australia, the Church is not at a historically strong or powerful moment. Catholic schools do not have an easy task in articulating and manifesting their Catholic identity. By no means is it facing an unprecedented crisis or low point. It does not, however, have limitless resources and energy. It must, therefore, give much thought as to how best to deploy its energies, bearing in mind that not all activities and new initiatives can be supported. Not all historic ministry and policy can be maintained. The Church must develop a strategic sense toward its pastoral ministry, and this has special relevance for Catholic schools.

Related to this guiding factor is a realisation that the expectations

---

5 Smith et al., *Lost in Transition*, 241.

about the role of schools in the new evangelisation should not be set at too high a level. The "terrain" for the new evangelisation in countries such as Australia is difficult. There is no strong prospect that this will change significantly in the foreseeable future. With this in mind, the contemporary discourse about Catholic schools in the third millennium must free itself from using the immediate pre-conciliar era as a constant reference point. This has both a positive and negative connotation.

The 1950s in many ways were a unique set of circumstances. Levels of Catholic practice and solidarity in this era were unusually high and should not be seen as normative. This was an era when religious socialisation was strong and the prevailing culture, in many ways, supported or did not challenge Christian norms. In another sense, the pre-conciliar era should not be regarded as some type of cultural prison from which Catholics emerged resolute never to return to again. Any religious group, and certainly one with the ancient roots of Catholicism, needs to make its history a strong aspect of its claims for plausibility. As Wuthnow puts it, "the church must …be backward looking; it has a special mission to preserve the past, to carry on a tradition.[6] The new evangelisation sits very well with a hermeneutic of continuity – where all eras have something to offer the contemporary Catholic. There are features of pre-conciliar Catholicism, by no means all, which can be used and incorporated into a legitimate worldview into the third millennium.

In developing some overriding principles for understanding the some of the implications of the new evangelisation for Catholic schools, my goal is to distill some practical wisdom from the preceding discussion. In doing this, I will make use of incidents and encounters during my many years as an educator working in Catholic schools.

---

6 Robert Wuthnow, *Christianity in the Twenty-First Century*. (New York: Oxford University Press, 1993), 48.

These are not intended to be empirical arguments but do illuminate several of the stated principles. As such, they serve, once again, as what Higgins calls a "type of micro-narrative," brief stories that are both dense and illustrative.[7]

As stated in the opening Chapter it is vital to see Catholic schools in contemporary culture as having role to play in evangelisation, but that this is not their sole or primary function. In many of these countries where the new evangelisation is especially pertinent, Catholic schools have long existed, and serve as part of the ecclesial structure of the Church. Catholic schools are not, however, primarily places of religious formation, focusing rather on the broader notion of the integral formation of the human person.[8] The preeminent place for such formation is the family. To be sure, this mission of Catholic schools has an evangelical aspect, but it needs to be placed in a wider context. This idea is expressed in the 1997 document of the Sacred Congregation for Catholic Education, *The Catholic School on the Threshold of the Third Millennium:*

> The Catholic school participates in the evangelising mission of the Church and is the privileged environment in which Christian education is carried out. In this way Catholic schools are at once places of evangelisation, of complete formation, of inculturation, of apprenticeship in a lively dialogue between young people of different religions and social backgrounds *(Section 11).*

My contention is that Catholic schools, mindful of cultural changes, and with sufficient human resources, a strong and reconceptualised religious education program, and a vigorous sense of their identity, can make a significant contribution to the new evangelisation.

---

7 Stephen H. Higgins, 'The Value of Anecdotal Evidence', in Lorne Tepperman and Harley Dickinson, (Eds), *Reading Sociology: Canadian Perspectives.* (New York: Oxford University Press, 2007), 11-16, at 11.
8 *The Catholic School.* Congregation for Catholic Education. Sydney: St Paul Publications.

(1) Human witness: The need for critical mass

In recent times there has been much comment on about how Catholic educational institutions can best configure themselves to cater for the radically changed cultural context within which they operate.[9] This type of discussion is, however, premised on an assumption that Catholic schools can rely on a critical mass of those associated with the institution to give credible and joyful witness to what they profess.[10] This notion is well captured in the 2008 Pastoral Letter of the Australian Catholic Bishops, *You Will be My Witnesses*.[11]

Catholic schools have always had a strong institutional presence in Australia and in many other places. An important part of this presence has been the strong witness of those associated with the school. This is an irreplaceable part of the "subterranean scaffolding" of Catholic schools.[12] In contemporary culture, however, questions of Catholic identity are compounded if Catholic educational institutions do not have sufficient numbers of individuals who give concrete witness to the goals and aspirations of the institution.[13] Perhaps the most important call for a quota of some sort is made in *Ex Corde Ecclesiae,* John Paul II's Constitution on Catholic universities. This proposes that "in order not to endanger the Catholic identity of the University

---

9 John Greene and John O'Keefe 2001 'Enrolment in Catholic Schools in the United States', in Nuzzi, R (Ed), *Handbook of Research on Catholic Education.* (Westport: Greenword, 2001),161-182. Maurice Ryan, 'Future Catholic Schools: Exclusive, Inclusive and Plural Options. *Journal of Religious Education,* 2008, 56(4), 21-28. Robert Schreiter, *The New Catholicity: Theology between the Global and the Local.* (Maryknoll: Orbis, 1997). Friedrich Schweitzer, 'From Plurality to Pluralism: Pluriform Identities and Religious Education'. *Journal of Religious Education,* 2007, 55(3), 3-8.
10 Adrian J. Walker, 'Rejoice Always. How Everyday Joy Responds to the Problem of Evil', *Communio* 31, Summer 2004, 200-235, at 201.
11 'You Will Be My Witnesses: A Pastoral Letter from the Catholic Bishops of Australia', June 22 2008. The letter concludes with the statement, "Let us boldly witness to our faith".
12 White, *Restoring Venice,* 184.
13 D. Paul Sullins, 'The Difference Catholic Makes: Catholic Faculty and Catholic Identity', *Journal for the Scientific Study of Religion,* 2004 43 (1) 83-101.

or Institute of Higher Studies, the number of non-Catholic teachers should not be allowed to constitute a majority within the Institution, which is and must remain Catholic."[14] The document by the bishops of NSW and the ACT, *Catholic Schools at the Crossroads,* acknowledges that Catholic schools of the future will "embrace changing enrolment patterns."[15] At the same time, it recognises the need for a critical mass of Catholic students and, perhaps more importantly, of Catholic leaders and staff, if schools are to retain a distinctively Catholic identity.[16] There is currently extensive discussion taking place on how to boost the Catholic enrolment in Catholic schools in Australia. White, for example, notes that the Catholic enrolment in Catholic schools in Tasmania is 56%, and the goal is to move towards a "critical mass" of 75%.[17] In their study of Catholic higher education, Morey and Piderit supported this notion when they contended:

> Most people in Catholic higher education circles shy away from numerical quotas, even as they acknowledge that Catholic institutional identity requires a critical mass of people who are knowledgeable about the Catholic traditions and as James Provost terms them, 'people who are in full communion'.[18]

If a Catholic school cannot point to a sizeable proportion, but by no means a majority, of those associated with the school community, who are animated by the Gospel and who see themselves as, in

---

14 Apostolic Constitution, on Catholic Universities, 1990, article 4, number 4. Obtained on 9/10/2008 from http://www.vatican.va/holy_father/john_paul_ii/apost_constitutions/documents/hf_jp-ii_apc_15081990_ex-corde-ecclesiae_en.html.
15 Pastoral Letter of the Bishops of NSW and the ACT, *Catholic Schools at a Crossroads,* 2007. Obtained on 14/1/2008 from www.cso.brokenbay.catholic.edu.au, 1-28, at 10.
16 *Catholic Schools at a Crossroads,* 12-18. The document also described schools as, among other things, centres of the new evangelisation. *Catholic Schools at a Crossroads,* 3.
17 White, *Restoring Venice.*
18 Melanie Morey and John Piderit, *Catholic Higher Education.* (New York: Oxford University Press, 2006), 226. The article referred to in the quotation is James Provost, 'The Sides of Catholic Identity' in John Wilcox and Irene King, (Eds), *Enhancing Religious Identity.* (Washington, D.C: Georgetown University Press, 2000), 23.

Pope John Paul II's term, disciples of Christ, then the justification of its Catholic identity is not straightforward.[19] These disciples are aside and separate from those who support the ethos of the school, and who maintain some type of loose association with the Church. Catholics of this type in contemporary culture exist in abundance. This is not a moral judgment, but an implication of the preceding analysis of the social and historical factors that have shaped the new evangelisation. Much scarcer, and increasingly so in the future, are Catholics who display a high level of commitment and who "do the work of religious groups."[20] A disproportionate number of these people are over the age of 55.[21]

As Braniff pointed out, a critical problem facing Catholic schools in Australia is the serious lack of committed Catholic teachers on staff, who are now far outweighed by non-Catholic and non-practising Catholics.[22] His conclusion is worth noting: "No matter how many coats of Marist or De La Salle varnish are applied to non-Catholic or non-practising Catholic staff, they are not, thereby, transformed into vibrant Marist or Catholic role-models for their students."[23] In the future, more institutions with historical Catholic association may need to closely examine their identity, especially if they are unable to point to a "critical mass" of individuals who are able to animate the identity of the institution.[24] When he was the secretary of the Congregation for Catholic Education, Michael Miller noted one of

---

19 Richard H. Parsons, 'Hiring for Mission: An Overview', *Conversations*, 1997, 12, Fall, 9-14.
20 Bibby, *Restless*, 105.
21 Robert E. Dixon, *The Catholic Community in Australia*. (Adelaide; Open Book Publishers, 2005), 57-64.
22 John Braniff, 'Charism and the Concept of a Catholic Education', *The Australasian Catholic Record*, 84(1), 2007, 22-34.
23 Braniff, *Charism*, 34. Murphy makes a similar point about faculty at Catholic universities. See Terence Murphy, *A Catholic University: Vision and Opportunities*. (Collegeville, Minn.: Liturgical Press, 2001), esp. 21-24.
24 Sullins, *Difference*, 100.

the consequences of this re-evaluation when quoting Benedict XVI:

> In the Holy Father's view, the measure of an institution can be judged by its Catholic integrity ... [if the institution secularises], it might be a matter of truth and justice that such an institution is no longer upheld ... [if] a Catholic institution is no longer motivated by a Catholic identity, it is better to let it go.[25]

Every effort must be made to recruit, in the terms of the arguments in this book, committed individuals into Catholic schools.[26] This is primarily the case for teachers and educational leaders but the same could be said for parents and students. This is not to say that there is no place for those who do not exhibit this commitment but it is a recognition that Catholic schools need people who are prepared to animate their religious dimension.[27] In a culture that in many ways encourages vicarious religious commitment, Catholic schools must be mindful that their employment policies reflect a strong desire to firstly recruit and then nurture teachers who can manifest and articulate their communion with the Church. The same can be said for parents and students in the school community. Catholic schools must ensure that they create an environment where religiously committed Catholics can feel that their needs and aspirations are being met. This in itself is not an evangelical task, but such a policy will help ensure that the environment within the school community is one that is conducive to an evangelical dimension being realised. Such an approach is not contrary to Catholic schools providing an educational option for other students most notably those with special needs, or who are economically disadvantaged. As with the staffing of the school what

---

25 Michael Miller, *Terrence Keeley Vatican Lecture at Notre Dame University*, October 31 2005. Obtained on 15/11/2007 at http://www.insidehighered.com/news/2005/11/03/catholic.

26 A similar point had been made by a number of Australian Catholic Educational leaders. For instance see White, *Restoring Venice*, Paul Sharkey.

27 Sullins, *Difference*, 100.

is critical here is the overall make-up of the student and parental body. It is an irreplaceable fillip to the evangelical aspect of the school if a strong cohort of committed Catholic staff, students and parents can give witness to the faith on which the school is premised.

(2) A need to revitalise and reconceptualise religious education

What is set out here is a broad overview of what can be called a new approach to religious education in Catholic schools. This is not intended to a comprehensive treatment, as this is beyond the scope of this book. Rather, what is set out here are some foundational principles that are harbingers of much future discussion, elaboration and reflection. The approach to religious education that will be spelled out here is primarily in response to the changed societal conditions in increasingly secular Western countries such as Australia. The situation, especially in the Catholic schools, is far different from even a few decades ago.

In the recent past, perhaps in reaction to the monolithic pre-concilar expression of Catholic culture, where teaching was passed on in a passive fashion, many in Catholic educational circles sought to better integrate experience and the foundational aspects of belief by encouraging a critical attitude to religious belief and practice. In this approach, the religious experience of individuals along with often passively acquired familial or societal religious beliefs were taken as a starting point. Very few today have an equivalent initial attitude. As such this new approach to religious education has a more evangelical dimension, since its primary focus is on a more proclamatory style in a cultural climate that challenges the very basis of religious belief. The foundation of religious education in Catholic schools remains, however, an educational one. What is outlined here is proposed as an educational model that best addresses the current cultural situation which Catholic schools face now, and will continue to face in the immediate future.

For many students in schools, their *a priori* position is that any type of strong religious belief is an untenable position. This awareness is one of the founding assumptions of what, in a wider context, Dulles has called "postcritical theology."[28] In addition, the religious experiences of students tend to be very weak. As an illustration of this, many of my students have, over the years, reported on the need for major supplementation of experiential models of religious education which require, in the first instance, some comment on a foundational event. Students in primary school, for example, may be doing a unit on baptism. As a legitimate first step, students are asked to recall baptisms that they have attended or to bring in some memento from their own baptism. The difficulty is that for many students this is just not possible. And as a result the teacher must provide a video, or something similar, of a baptism to provide the initial experience.

On a deeper level, the prevailing culture tends to contest all truth claims so the very notion of religious positions based on normative truth claims is considered to be untenable. Aidan Nichols expressed this concern well: "When, as now, cognitive skepticism about morals and faith tends to rule, it is important to show how firm epistemic commitments in these areas may still be responsible human acts."[29] A postmodern consciousness is well attuned to deconstruction of meaning. What is needed is an approach to religious education that builds up meaning principally by seeing connections in what appear

28 Avery Dulles, *The Craft of Theology: From Symbol to System.* (New York: Crossroad, 1995), 3-17.
29 Aidan Nichols, 'Avery Dulles: Theologian in the Church', *Chicago Studies,* 2008, 47(2), 135-155.

to be unrelated areas and also by exposure to truth claims.[30] This is a difficult, challenging, and, to some extent, counter-cultural task. A person with a number of options, and no compelling reason to choose any particular one, wants to hear what is on offer. The new evangelisation implies that Catholics have something to offer in a religious marketplace that is competitive and highly diverse. If we accept the notion that one way of looking at individuals in countries such as Australia is to see them as religious consumers, then a number of consequences follow. As consumers, in a fractured postmodern milieu, they have abundant choices, including the popular choice of becoming or remaining loosely affiliated, and are not easily compelled into action. Religious groups then can only rely on persuasion, rather than coercion or socialisation, to get their messages across.[31] For religious education in Catholic schools, one implication of this new emphasis is giving careful consideration to what Catholicism has to offer, or to put this in propositional terms, what answers Catholicism offers.[32]

Having an answer

> We are letting them down, sending many, and probably most, of them out into the world without the basic intellectual tools and most basic formation needed to think and express even the most elementary of reasonably defensible moral thoughts and claims. And that itself, we think, is morally wrong.

---

30 Anthony Kelly, *An Expanding Theology: Faith in a World of Connections.* (Newton, Australia: E.J. Dwyer, 1993).

31 Mason and his colleagues make a similar point, Mason, *Gen Y*, 338. See also RM 30.1.

32 A similar emphasis is given in Pope Benedict XVI Apostolic Letter to launch the Year of Faith, beginning in October of 2012 to mark the fiftieth anniversary of the opening of the Second Vatican Council. He drew attention to the need to make a "concerted effort to rediscover and study the fundamental contents of the faith. Apostolic letter *Motu Proprio Data, Porta Fidei*, section 11. Obtained on 23/10/11 from http://www.vatican.va/holy_father/benedict_xvi/motu_proprio/documents/hf_ben-xvi_motu-proprio_20111011_porta-fidei_en.html

The quote above from a book by Smith et al., on emerging adults makes a very strong point about the need, or rather the obligation, of the great institutions of society to do a much better job in forming young people. The sentiment expressed here can be extrapolated to religious education in Catholic schools, as the discipline seeks to develop a new mentality that is cognisant of some of the principles of the new evangelisation.

A brief recollection here tries to encapsulate a mentality that should pervade Catholic schools, but which has special relevance to a new approach to religious education. This mentality is a response to the religious culture that has emerged in many of the countries to which the new evangelisation is addressed. A number of years ago, I attended Mass in a parish conducted by a religious order. On this occasion a young visiting Swedish priest of the order was concelebrating with one of the older resident Australian priests. During the homily the older priest made the point, and this could be considered almost a generational refrain – that the Church's mission centred on getting people to ask the right questions. At the conclusion of Mass, after being thanked and acknowledged, the visiting priest added a telling and bold rejoinder. He commented, noting the homily, that the Church as well as stimulating questions, should also provide answers. He added people in Sweden have enough questions, but they will listen to someone who has some answers.

Sweden is a country that, perhaps better than any other, embodies the notion of vicarious religion. So a "safety net" is in place. It has a very small Catholic minority. Why should anyone in Sweden, or more to the point Australia, listen to a religious group that does not have a distinct message, a clear and cogent sense of its own identity and mission, and the confidence to provide answers and a direction in life?[33] Catholic schools – and the preeminent place to do this is in religious education – need to be able to provide an answer as to why people today should be religious in a manner that moves well beyond the passive acceptance of vicarious religion in all its manifestations.

The Christian answer can resonate deeply with human aspirations. For instance, one manifestation of the consumerist approach to religion is the trivialisation of relationships and sexuality. Many younger people in contemporary culture are uncomfortable with what has been described as the hook-up culture.[34] This is verified in much recent research on young adults. Regnerus and Uecker, for instance note ten myths about sex and relationships amongst university-aged students, which can easily be extrapolated to high school students.[35] The refutation of these myths equates very well with the Catholic view on sexuality, relationships and marriage.[36] What is needed is more thinking around the question, "How best can Catholics, and in particular Catholic schools, articulate counter cultural messages such as this?"

As Max Weber points out, humans have a need both to see the world and their place in it as meaningful.[37] Religions in general, and Catholic schools in particular, are well placed to provide what Bouma identifies as one core driver of society, namely "hope and meaning grounded in a connection with that which is more than passing,

33 The 2007 Catholic Almanac puts the Catholic population of Sweden at 149,000 or 1.6% of the total. Matthew, E. Bunson, 2007 *Catholic Almanac*. (Huntingdon, IN.: Our Sunday Visitor, 2006), 328.
34 Kathleen Bogle, *Hooking Up: Sex, Dating and Relationships on Campus*. (New York: New York University, 2008).
35 Mark Regnerus and Jeremy Uecker, *Premarital Sex in America: How Young Americans Meet, Mate, and Think About Marrying*. (New York: Oxford University Press, 2011).
36 The congruence between overcoming the ten myths and what I would call a Catholic sensibility is well worth noting, see Regnerus and Uecker, *Premarital Sex*, 236-249. To note just three: Myth One, "long-term exclusivity is a fiction"; Myth Six, "porn won't affect your relationships; Myth Ten, "moving in together is definitely a step toward marriage", 249.
37 Max Weber, *Sociology of Religion*. (Boston: Beacon Press, 1963), 23-49.

partial and broken".[38] To have firm, ready and engaging answers – and this is not just a cognitive reality, but implies a whole human experience – is not to be a fundamentalist or to peddle simplistic nostrums. It is responding in a Pauline way to the task of evangelising both individuals and culture.

Search for truth and meaning: content driven religious education

A philosophical basis for religious education in Catholic schools should be rooted in epistemologies that see knowledge as something which is not only constructed, but in its essence as something which is discovered. Dulles has suggested that an epistemology inspired by the work of Polanyi has much to offer Catholic theologians who wish to provide a justification for truth claims.[39] Such an approach also has implications for educators working in Catholic schools, since it is based on the notion that truth, in the broad sense, is arrived at not through a process of construction, as something that is discovered, usually not in an instant but in a gradual movement akin to a picture coming into focus.[40] This type of epistemological thinking is well established in philosophical systems that are well represented in the Catholic tradition. Indeed one of the most powerful accounts of the role of truth in philosophy, from its Aristotelian origins to modern fragmentation, is given in Ratzinger's *Introduction to Christianity* first published in 1965.[41] The search for truth transforms the primary epistemological basis of religious education from a hermeneutic that seeks to reconcile the Christian story with the experience of the person achieved through praxis, toward a sense of encountering the great questions of life. The key question, therefore, becomes not how

---

38 Bouma, *Australian Soul*, 205.
39 Avery Dulles, Faith, Church and God: Insights from Michael Polanyi. *Theological Studies*, 1984, 45, 531-546.
40 Avery Dulles, *The Communication of Faith and its Contents*. (Washington D.C.: NCEA)
41 Joseph Ratzinger, *Introduction to Christianity*. (San Francisco: Ignatius press, 1990).

does religious education in Catholic schools help students construct meaning, but how does it assist them to discover truth? By framing the question in this way, a number of consequences follow which, in total, change the research conversation about the structure of religious education, especially its pedagogical dimension.

A key aspect of this new approach is a strong commitment to a content driven, pedagogically sound religious education. A more content driven religious education is focused on presenting materials to students in a systematic, ordered and engaging way. A key consideration here is what is to be included in a religious education course of studies. Implicit here are judgments about what the critical content areas are and what are less important topics. The content to be covered must be both sequential and spiralled, giving students exposure to a cogent development of topics, where key ideas are covered more than once in the curriculum. The consequences of not following this approach are well captured by Ratzinger writing in 1983:

> The renunciation of a structured, fundamental schema for transmitting the faith, drawing upon tradition in its entirety, resulted in a fragmentation of the faith presentation, which not only abetted arbitrariness, but also simultaneously called into question the seriousness of the individual elements of the content, which belong to a whole and, when detached from it, appear haphazard and incoherent.[42]

As Smith and Denton put it, "parents and faith communities should not be shy about teaching teens ... there seems to be a curious reluctance among many adults to teach teens when it comes to

---

42 Joseph Ratzinger, *Handing on the Faith in an Age of Disbelief.* (San Francisco: Ignatius Press, 1983), 15.

faith".[43] This is just not a cognitive process. The message must be delivered with authenticity and conviction.[44] And it does have some similarity to what Dulles has called for as a more apologetic style of religious education. Apologetics here does not have the connotation of something defensive and inward looking. Rather it is a response to new circumstances where religious groups are required to provide a clear and cogent sense of what they have to offer and how this meets both human aspirations and divine mandate. It also recognises that one very pertinent assumption the educators in Catholic schools can make, is that most of their audiences will not be easily swayed by arguments that are grounded in references to Church authority and which do not respect the lived experience of students. Dulles summarises this approach well when he writes, "the Christian interpretation of life, based on the biblical narrative, is not presented as obvious and irresistible, but as incomparably more meaningful and profound than alternative interpretations."[45]

Paul VI, in *Evangelii Nuntiandi*, expresses the need for Catholics to be able to give a cogent justification for their lives. This is especially important in a culture where choice and options abound and no one meta-narrative is dominant.

> Even the finest witness will prove ineffective in the long run if it is not explained, justified – what Peter called always "having

---

43 Smith and Denton, *Soul*, 267. Dulles adds that younger Catholics need to be "challenged with the hard truths of the gospel", Avery Dulles, 'Vatican II: Substantive Teaching: A Reply to John W. O'Malley and others', *America*, 2003, March 21, 17.
44 Allan Figueroa Deck, Evangelisation as a Conceptual Framework for the Church's Mission: The Case of U.S. Hispanics, in Thomas P. Rausch, (Ed) *Evangelising America*. (New York: Paulist Press, 2004), 85-11 at 105. See also Gallagher, *Symbols*, 126-127. Mason, *Gen Y*, 340-341. A more critical perspective on ministry from the front is given in David Ranson, *Across the Great Divide: Bridging Spirituality and Religion Today*. (Strathfield, NSW: St Paul's, 2002), esp. 16-37.
45 Avery Dulles, *The Communication of Faith and its Content*. (Washington D.C.: National Catholic Educational Association, 1985), 11.

your answer ready for people who ask you the reason for the hope that you all have" – and made explicit by a clear and unequivocal proclamation of the Lord Jesus.[46]

Highlighting the distinctiveness of Catholicism, which will be discussed in greater detail in the next section, also has a religious education dimension. Those involved in religious education could do much to promote a distinct Catholic identity.[47] Hoge and his colleagues point out that in the recent past, emphasis on teaching about the distinctive features of Catholicism has diminished.[48] If young people, especially, do not hear about these aspects of the faith tradition, it is unlikely that they will be able to understand and incorporate a strong Catholic sensibility into their lives.

> [There are] negative consequences of a religious education that emphasises ecumenism and a common Christian heritage but fails to include a focus on what is distinctive about being Catholic and why that matters. To continue this generic orientation will have detrimental consequences to the future of the Church.[49]

Role of the religious education teacher

There is no question that significant demands are placed on religious education (RE) teachers in this new conceptualisation of religious education. This is a good manifestation of an underlying principle, namely, that the new evangelisation in Catholic schools is not an easy and straightforward task. A critical part of this role is an enhanced emphasis on the role of the witness provided by the RE teacher. This is a particular manifestation of the need for a critical mass of committed people in Catholic schools. Benedict XVI powerfully reminds us of the need for authenticity when he commented,

---

46 EN, 22.
47 James D. Davidson, Ed, *The Search for Common Ground: What Unites and Divides Catholic Americans.* (Huntington, IN.: Our Sunday Visitor, 1997), 93-111.
48 Hoge et al., *Young Adult*, 231-235.
49 Hoge et al., *Young Adult*, 232.

"Educators of the faith cannot run the risk of looking like some sort of clown, who is simply playing a role".[50] For many years, I have worked with prospective teachers, and especially RE teachers, who plan to work in Catholic schools. A constant issue in that time has been the tension between providing enough teachers to staff the system and the requirement that RE teachers in particular have specialist qualifications that will enable them to teach religion in an academically sound fashion. Whilst it may not always be the case with religious education, there is no question that in terms of realising the new evangelisation in schools, RE teachers need to have strong content knowledge, professional skills, and to be prepared to witness to what they teach. To fail to acknowledge this is to misunderstand the demands that the new evangelisation places on Catholic schools and set schools up for failure by demanding of them something that they cannot deliver.

In order to be able to respond to the questions of students living in a secular culture and to teach in an integrated and educationally sophisticated way, RE teachers in Catholic schools must display substantial content knowledge and be able to convey this in a systematic manner. If they do not have this it is like the blind leading the blind.[51] This encompasses not only the traditional areas of religious education such as theology and scripture, but also a good grasp of what are predominately philosophical and pedagogical issues. For example, many students today may raise concerns about the classical Christian conception of God. This involves not a distant cosmic energy, but a personal, loving and what Augustine called a simple God about whom we can know something but who will

---

50 Address of Benedict XVI on *Commemoration of St Ambrose of Milan*, Zenit News Service, 24/10/07.
51 Dulles, *Communication of Faith*, 16.

always be beyond total human comprehension.[52] The RE teacher should convey this understanding in a fashion that reflects the learning needs of the child and as part of an integrated approach to covering the essential features of the Christian message. In this way, religious education can be seen as an interrelated whole and not a series of unrelated fragments. One of the key roles of the teacher is to be able, in the first instance, to synthesise for themselves a mature understanding of the Christian message, and to then to pass on this understanding to students in a coherent fashion.

Focus on Pedagogy

A new approach to religious education involves a much stronger emphasis on pedagogy which has a range of practical implications. There needs to be recognition that religious education in Catholic schools is a discipline which needs ongoing support. This requires effort, planning, and discernment, and is dependent of the quality of religious education teachers. If the goal of religious education is to provide a clear and cogent presentation of the Catholic vision as a basis for future dialogue and learning then how this is achieved becomes a critical issue. This is fundamentally a pedagogical issue. That is, how can the teaching and learning that goes on in religious education classes be more effective and student focused? This appears to be a simple consideration but it can often be neglected in the discussion of how to improve the quality of religious education in Catholic schools.

To take two examples of the questions posed by a more pedagogical focus in religious education, consider the following. Firstly, how do we teach young people about the Christian concept of God when the prevailing culture seeks to reduce to God to a type of ineffable generic force in the universe? Secondly, how do we best convey a

---

52 Rymarz, R. and McClarney, G. (2011) 'Teaching about Augustine: Providing a Scaffolding for Learning', *Journal of Adult Theological Education*.

sense of conscience and moral action as arising from fundamental conceptions of the human person, and not as something that is contingent merely on the person and the circumstances they find themselves in? These questions do have a philosophical aspect to them, but in terms of the work of religious education teachers, a more critical issue is how do we convey in a clear and coherent fashion the core beliefs of the tradition on these and similar issues? In models of religious education that place emphasis on the process to be followed, the hard issues of how best to present challenging content can be overlooked. In a more content-driven model the focus is on what content to present, and how best to present this to students.

(3) Celebrate the distinctiveness of Catholicism

As part of their contribution to the new evangelisation, Catholic schools need to place greater emphasis on the distinctive features of Catholic belief and practice, and in doing so create places where genuine evangelisation can occur.[53] This is part of what Bouma saw as a general trend by religious groups to "reexamine their core beliefs and declaring their distinctiveness."[54] The need for a greater emphasis on the distinctive features of Catholicism is primarily driven by a changed cultural landscape where Churches in general, and schools in particular need to move away from a monopolistic stance where many adherents moved into faith communities as a result of socialisation and other passive factors. Young people, in particular, have a number of options and will most likely be attracted to groups which, amongst

---

53 One such distinctive practice is devotion to the Sacred Heart of Jesus. Prendergast argues that this should be revived as "the most complete expression of Christian religion." Terence Prendergast, 'The Sacred Heart Devotion' in John M. McDermott and John Gavin (Eds), *Pope John Paul II on the Body: Human Eucharistic and Ecclesial, Festschrift Avery Cardinal Dulles, S.J.* (Philadelphia: Saint Joseph's University Press, 2007), 387-391. For a different view on its relevance see, Cashen, *Sacred Heart*, 215-219.

54 Bouma, *Australian Soul*, 146. He goes on to note that "this can be done harshly like Sydney-side Anglicans ... or simply firmly and confidently."

other things, have a clear and coherent identity and can communicate this effectively. The new evangelisation is a positive response to a much more difficult cultural milieu for religious groups and can be seen as a reemphasis of a fundamental missionary identity. Schools that have this mentality almost inevitably develop a strong self-identity, and one way this is manifested is proclamation of such distinctive features as being at the heart of its self-conception.

The Catholic identity of schools needs to be strengthened across the board. This should not be undertaken as a type of triumphalism, but in the sense of being proud of a culture and a heritage. Many groups in contemporary Australia are quite rightly trying to recapture something of their cultural and spiritual heritage. Catholic schools could also be part of this movement. This is one way of establishing the boundaries that give any group its cohesiveness and purpose. Reestablishing boundaries is, however, difficult. In recognition of this, a first step could be preserving those distinctive Catholic features which still exist in schools.[55] The challenge to maintain and establish boundaries that mark them as distinct from secular groups faces all mainstream Christian Churches. The boundaries which mark the Catholic identity of schools also needs to be maintained. The Catholic identity of schools can be defined in comparatively broad, non-distinctive, terms.[56] Many of these could be applied to other groups.[57] This is not to say that they are not valid indicators. In the

---

55 Greeley, *Revolution*, 137.
56 Thomas H. Groome, *What Makes Us Catholic: Eight Gifts for Life*. (San Francisco: Harper, 2003).
57 Gray provides anther illustration of an expansive but not distinctive definition of Catholic identity. She lists the following as markers of Catholic identity: the wealth of the tradition; concern for the disadvantaged – social justice; saramentality; the deep practicality, ordinariness of faith; faith of women; constant challenge of God's hope for us – eschatological orientation; Janette Gray, *Singing from the Same Hymn Sheet-Is this our Understanding of Catholic Identity Today?*, Paper delivered at National Catholic Education Conference, July 2006, Sydney.

current era, however, as opposed to the immediate post-conciliar time, a reemphasis of the distinctive features of Catholic identity, over and above generic descriptors, may be in order.[58] At the centre of this distinctiveness should a strong Christocentric tone. This is in keeping with Moule's point, "At no point within the New Testament is there any evidence that the Christian stood for an original philosophy of life or an original ethic. Their sole function was to bear witness to what they claim as an event – the rising of Jesus from the dead".[59]

(4) Segmented Ministry: Creating community and spaces for the New Evangelisation

Catholic schools exist in a wider societal context, where strong religious convictions are marginalised. A critical awareness in Catholic schools, embracing the new evangelisation, is to recognise this cultural context and to take steps to create a context where religious commitment is recognised, valued and respected as a legitimate option. Students are very sensitive to issues such as these and as a general principle Catholic schools must be seen as a place where students can, if they wish, be religiously involved at a level above the community norm. A first step in this direction is to adopt a multifaceted, or segmented, approach to pastoral ministry and outreach. The new evangelisation in schools would be greatly enhanced if schools could point to groups

---

58 Groome argues that we cannot distinguish Catholicism on the basis of what is unique to it as, "the only candidate for something truly unique to Roman Catholicism is the Petrine office". One assumes here that Groome is speaking about what distinguishes Roman Catholicism from other Orthodox faiths. The critical point is, however, how Catholicism distinguishes itself from the wider culture. There is a much firmer basis for this then just the papacy. Groome, *What Makes Us Catholic*, 31.

59 C.F.D. Moule, *The Phenomenon of the New Testament*. (London, 1967), 14. Quoted in Bernard Lonergan, 'The Future of Christianity' in William F. Ryan and Bernard J. Tyrell (Eds), *A Second Collection*. (London: Darton, Longman & Todd, 1974), 156. Lonergan himself adds, "What distinguishes the Christian then is not God's grace, which he shares with others, but mediation of God's grace through Jesus Christ our Lord", Ryan and Tyrell, *Second Collection*, 156.

within the school which actively support those who seek to deepen their faith. In the current cultural milieu, such groups would not appeal to all, but if Bauman's analysis of postmoderntity is correct, then we can be assured that there will be some students who feel the need to find peer support for their religious questions. A point that can be overlooked in Bauman's argument is that the social impact of postmodernity, especially on younger people is largely negative – a point reinforced by Smith and his colleagues in their analysis of those in transition to adulthood.[60] The alienation from others brings with it a transitory and disconnected style of life. The new evangelisation in a broad sense can offer an alternative to these feelings by providing a sense of community and fellowship between people who share similar beliefs or aspirations.

The cultural milieu which was elaborated on in previous chapters tends to underplay the significance of religion. The advantage of this for schools who seek to actualise the new evangelisation is that students do not, in the main, bring with them negative or overtly hostile feelings toward religious expression. In keeping with the motif of younger people being religious consumers, they are open to proposals that seem to them to be attractive and offering something that is not available elsewhere. An essential aspect of religion as Stark, and others remind us of is that it offers the opportunity of an exchange with the gods. Presented in an appealing fashion, this may be attractive to a range of younger people. At the same time it is important to state that a fundamental understanding of the new evangelisation in Catholic schools is to realise that it is a difficult program to bring to realisation. Initiatives such as student-centred, extracurricular faith based groups may not appeal to a large numbers of students. But this is no reason for discouragement, but a call to provide a rich experience.

---

60 Smith et al., *Lost in Transition*, 49.

The recollection of a graduate student of mine illustrates this idea. She was a teacher who was actively involved in sponsoring a prayer group that seemed to encapsulate well the principle of segmented ministry in schools (it also is an example of being prepared to try something new, a principle that will be discussed in greater detail in the following section). She realised that most of the students' interests lay elsewhere, but over the years a prayer group developed that had good links with the surrounding parishes. Most importantly, it had become the place in the school which attracted students who for whatever reason wanted to learn more about the Catholic faith. She recounted the testimony of a former student who now herself was studying to be a teacher. The girl had first come to the prayer group to learn more about the faith that so much animated her grandmother. Prayer, both private and communal, was an important part of the grandmother's life, and the girl wanted to explore this as a portal into learning more about the Catholicism that was unpractised in her own life. Here we see an instance of the new evangelisation in schools in action. A number of factors have converged, but the key in this story is a specific group within the school that provides support, fellowship and encouragement.

Being part of a supportive community is a vital aspect of sustaining religious plausibility in contemporary culture.[61] It also speaks to a very human need to be part of a group which professes similar beliefs, goals and with whom one feels comfortable.[62] A feature of the post-conciliar landscape is a loss of a sense of community amongst many Catholics but most significantly amongst younger ones. Grassroots supportive communities have long been associated with Catholic communal life. The new evangelisation is dependent on

---

61 Kavanaugh, *Following Christ*, 147.
62 Mark McCrindle and Mark Beard, *Seriously Cool, Marketing and Communicating with Diverse Generations*. (Baulkham Hills: McCrindle Research), 2006.

the existence or reanimation of active communities that can provide support to those already someway on their journey of faith and, more importantly, to those who are looking to become more committed.

For most people the primary community of faith is the family. Another community of faith is the parish. Schools cannot replace either families or parishes as place of catechesis or evangelisation but they can contribute something in both areas by providing opportunities for communities of faith to form.[63] These supportive groups would have much in common with the notion of moral communities.[64] Moral communities are formative in the sense that they provide support for individuals to live out beliefs and a certain pattern of behaviour. Members of moral communities feel, in the first instance accountable to each other.

Due to the large amount of time that most young people spend at school a supportive network here could play a valuable role in providing peer ministry. People who gather here have much in common and are at a stage of life where major life decisions are less likely to have been made. If communities such as these could form in Catholic schools then a place where the new evangelisation could occur has been established. In a sense what is being proposed is an answer to the question posed in the preface to this book. When my friend and I discussed all those years ago what we would do if someone came up to us and wanted to know more about Catholicism, our best response would have been something like, "go over to this group they meet every … night and support each other and are really keen to nurture people who are seeking a closer relationship with God through the Catholic Church." None of this is supposed to run contrary to work of parishes or diocesan based youth programs. Indeed they seem to run in parallel, where each can support each other.

---

63 Paul Wilkes, *Excellent Catholic Parishes.* (New York: Paulist Press, 2001).
64 Stark.

Also implicit in the new evangelisation is a certain fudging of the traditional distinctions between evangelisation, catechesis and education. To be sure, under the classical description, what is occurring in such faith-based moral communities in schools is catechesis, that is, the cultivation of faith that has to some extent been owned by the individual. The new evangelisation at its core calls for an evangelisation of those who have already been baptised, but who are living a life removed from the Gospel. Supportive groups provide a venue where this reengagement, or even initial engagement, can occur. It may well be brought to fruition at some later stage in a different setting, but at least the initial contact has been made.

Another possibility in providing experiences of supportive communities, which may augment more ongoing structures are intense, episodic experiences of community. School retreats are already a successful example of this type of experience, but they could be supported by a best practice model of outreach ministry.[65] This is where students from a number of schools in a region or district are invited to come together and given the strong experience of liturgy, teaching and fellowship. This differs from the retreat experience which tends to involve all students. What is proposed here is a smaller, differentiated dedicated gathering which is offered in addition to the standard school retreats. In a way, such "best practice" models have some similarities with the experience of pilgrims at World Youth Day (WYD).[66]

---

65 Rachelle Tullio, and Graham Rossiter, 'Critical Issues for the Future of Senior Class Retreats in Australian Catholic Schools: Part 1 – Major Theoretical and Educational Issues'. *Journal of Religious Education* 57.4 (2009): 57-70. 'Securing the Future of Live-In Retreats in Australian Catholic Secondary Schools: Part 2 Psychological and Spiritual Issues Related to the Nature, Purposes and Conduct of Retreats.' *Journal of Religious Education* 58.2 (2010): 65-74.
66 Richard Rymarz, 'Who goes to World Youth Day: Some Data on Under 18 Australian Pilgrims', *Journal of Beliefs and Values*, 2007, 28 (1).

One of the features of WYD is that it creates a safe space in which religious identity can be explored. Many Catholic youth who do not have a strong religious attachment, and others wishing to explore Catholicism further, lack a suitable forum for such exploration. For such students designated camps could provide such a structure. It is far easier to deal with religious questions in a concrete form rather than an abstraction. For those youth in Catholic schools who are interested in learning more about Catholicism, a directed camp program could be one service the school could offer which facilitates this questioning. This is not in opposition to the work of parishes, but if younger people are not associated with parishes then a reasonable strategy is to establish contact with younger people where they can be found, that is, in schools.

In such a proposal it needs to be stressed that such "best practice" camps are something that schools could offer to students. There is no sense here that these are compulsory or necessary for students to attend. At the same time, they could incorporate follow up with parish based youth ministry or other similar groups. Such camps do not replace the need for a strong religious education program in the school, which remains one of the keystones of the new evangelisation in Catholic schools. The religious education program is aimed, however, at the whole student body and has a strong educational focus.

Gathering interested students from across Catholic schools together for a relatively short period of time even on a yearly basis seems to be a suitable response to the challenges of post modernity; but in fact this type of Christian outreach is well established. To give one example, one of the most significant aspects of Romano Guardini's ministry was the time he spent as a leading figure in the *Quickborn* (wellsprings of life) youth movement in pre-war Germany.[67] A key

---

67 Krieg, *Precursor*, 21-23.

part of this organisation were summer camps held at *Burg Rothenfels am Main*. These attracted university students who were interested in deepening their Christian commitment in the style offered.[68] As well as Guardini, other prominent mentors attended, and the participants experienced excellent preaching, innovative liturgy, a variety of cultural and spiritual pursuits and strong fellowship. Rather than being seen as competition to conventional parish life, this type of focused ministry provides revitalisation for the group, who attend and then return to more conventional modes of faith expression.[69]

In conclusion, new ways of cooperation between schools and parishes should be investigated and supported. If we base the initial stages of the new evangelisation to youth on those who already have some connection with the faith community, then a critical consideration is how to build up a sufficiently large number who can provide the type of peer support often lacking in their faith development. This situation would be greatly enhanced if schools and parishes worked together to overcome the problem of having only relatively few young people involved in certain areas. It would also make the delivery of supportive services far more effective. There may be some possibility of establishing formal links between schools and parishes. One means, for example, could be youth ministers who work both in parishes and in schools.

(5) Reach out to parents and be prepared to try new strategies

Anything that Catholic schools can do to strengthen the role of the family in its role as seedbed and nurturer of faith would greatly assist

---

68 Karl Rahner was one of the many young adults deeply influenced by their attendance at these intensive summer camps. Fergus Kerr, *Twentieth-Century Catholic Theologians: From Neoscholasticism to Nuptial Mysticism*. (Malden, Ma: Blackwell, 2007), 87.
69 Dulles offers the idea of "novitiates for life" as a basis for training lay leaders in the community of disciples. These are "brief gatherings for spiritual renewal are a great help toward achieving authentic discipleship in the Church". Dulles, *Models*, 219.

the new evangelisation. This all-encompassing mandate is simply recognition of the unique and irreplaceable role the family plays in faith formation, and as the bedrock of society.[70] As a means of reaching out to parents who have lost a sense of faith, or have even drifted a long way from the Church ministry to families, this is an area of great potential. If we work from the general principle that most parents are very interested in activities that will help them get closer to their children and improve their lives, the challenge for the new evangelisation is to convince parents that getting closer to Christ will help their relationships with their children and also make their children's lives better. In the initial stages this type of ministry may not attract large numbers but is a task worth preserving with. This idea is illustrated by an example from my teaching experience.

I was once commissioned to run four sessions for parents who were interested in nurturing the faith of their teenage children. These sessions, along with many others, were coordinated through the Catholic Education Office in a large Archdiocese. All sessions were free and information about them was circulated to parents via Catholic schools. The first three sessions were cancelled for lack of registrations. The fourth one went ahead, largely as an act of solidarity for the three parents who had registered previously, then registered for this one once the earlier sessions were cancelled. Parents who attended expressed their concern at the difficulties they faced as faith mentors to their children, they also spoke of other parents, friends and acquaintances who were similarly concerned and trying to stem the tide of what they saw as a hostile culture. The organisers considered this exercise to be a major disappointment, one that would not be offered in next year's calendars of activities.

---

70 This was a constant theme of John Paul, for example in *Ecclesia Europa*, he wrote: "The Church in Europe at every level must faithfully proclaim anew the truth about marriage and the family", EE, 90.

The focus of this activity, as well as the target group, both fall within the principles of the new evangelisation in Catholic schools. Parents who want to support the faith development of their children are an appropriate audience and assisting them is not a superfluous enterprise. The attendance at the seminar offered here was low, but it does beg the question that if marriage education courses were made optional how many would attend? There could be a number of reasons for the apparent lack of interest. These would include practical issues such as the difficulty some people have in attending any meetings or seminars in the evening. Perhaps more significantly it needs to be realised that many parents are relatively uninterested in the faith development of their children. In the main, they are content with what is currently being offered. This is not a moral judgment, but a descriptive one that tries to explain why the new evangelisation, at least in its initial stages, may not attract numerically strong responses.

Certainly a generalised invitation issued through the school will not attract most parents. At the same time, using other more personal means of communication could boost the number of parents attending. In the scenario, a number of attendees know of other parents who would be interested. Extending this idea, in addition to schools sending home a flyer to all, some parents who might be more predisposed to the activity could be contacted individually by a phone call or personalised letter informing them of the event. This type of communication depends on Catholic institutions such as schools having more than a cursory association with members of the school community and knowing something of the background of each family in the school.

The new evangelisation is a difficult task. It is worthwhile to recall Ratzinger's remark here, about success not being one of the names of God. Those engaged in it, therefore, must be prepared to try new strategies to help promote it and to be aware that some of these may fail. To stay within the framework of the scenario above, thinking outside the conventional is to be encouraged. Questions such as the following can be asked: "Is this an opportunity for cooperation with the school and parish?" "Can we try to identify other groups which run similar programs and use some of their skills?" "In particular, do Evangelical churches have models for parental formation that we could adapt or use?" "Does the school have structures in place which would enable parents interested in assisting the faith development of their children to gather and offer each other support?" These questions are not meant to be exhaustive but to be indicative of a mentality that seeks to enlarge and engage the scope of the new evangelisation.

The new evangelisation sets itself high goals, and as a result can often lead to what seems to be disappointment. But with high goals comes the possibility of high returns, and these are not always best measured in gross numbers. As Wilson points out, using Augustine as a model, conversion in the post modern world is a dynamic process that engages the whole person and needs to seen in individual terms and not as a mass movement.[71] In terms of the seminars for parents, six parents attended. If we double this number to account for the friends and colleagues that those who attended mentioned as being interested this gives us 12. If we were to use some of the communication ideas raised earlier, in the whole of this very large school system then 20 more might be added as a conservative estimate. This would leave us with an audience of 32. Say that each parent attending has 2.5 children on average. This means that 80 or so people will be reached in some way by the seminar. This is not a large number but it is not insignificant. The purpose of this crude arithmetic is to show that

---

71 Phillip Wilson, 'Shaping the Future of the Church', *Origins*, 2007, 78, 37-41, at 40.

with some planning and a proportionate sense of the likely outreach of the program what was considered a marginal activity can become quite sustainable. The key point is not to be overawed by numbers or lack of them. What is more important are the activity and the audience.

The new strategies in Catholic schools that are anticipated by the new evangelisation may not all be successful. This is not a reflection of the futility of the task, rather of its difficulty. It is important to maintain a responsible consciousness in these endeavours. Implementers of the new evangelisation in Catholic schools need to be convinced that by being attentive, intelligent and rational that they can effect a course of action that will be fruitful at least, on its own terms, and in due course. As Lonergan puts it, "concern for the future will work itself out by human means, by drawing on human experience, human intelligence, human judgment, human decision but again this is quite compatible with a profoundly religious attitude".[72]

Concluding Comments

In discussing a concept such as the new evangelisation of Pope John Paul II and its applications and relevance to Catholic schools in increasingly secular Western countries there is tendency to get lost on the scale of the discussion. I would like, therefore, to draw this Chapter and the book as a whole to a conclusion by repeating a summative idea that was introduced at the beginning of this chapter.

My contention is that Catholic schools, mindful of cultural changes, and with sufficient human resources, a strong and reconceptualised religious education program and a vigorous sense of their identity, can make a significant contribution to the new evangelisation as

---

72 Bernard Lonergan, 'The Absence of God in Modern Culture' in William F. Ryan and Bernard J. Tyrell (Eds), *A Second Collection*. (London: Darton, Longman & Todd, 1974), 109-115.

envisaged by Pope John Paul II. The new evangelisation is best seen as a response to the place of the Church in a particular societal reality. This new context calls for renewed sense of mission in the Church as a whole. Catholic schools have a role to play in this mission. By giving students a lived experience of a Catholic community, one that engages the mind as well as the affective dimension and is mindful of its own identity, Catholic schools can respond authentically to new cultural demands. To be sure, this is difficult, since it requires constant and sustained effort. This evangelistic dimension of Catholic schools cannot be assumed and must be striven for with constant purpose and resolute determination.

* * *

CPSIA information can be obtained at www.ICGtesting.com
Printed in the USA
LVOW11s1632270116

472516LV00002B/349/P